50 Tomato-Inspired Dish Recipes for Home

By: Kelly Johnson

Table of Contents

- Classic Marinara Sauce
- Caprese Salad
- Margherita Pizza
- Tomato Basil Soup
- Bruschetta
- Stuffed Tomatoes
- Tomato Risotto
- Tomato and Mozzarella Panini
- Gazpacho
- Ratatouille
- Tomato Confit
- Tomato Tart
- Tomato and Goat Cheese Galette
- Tomato Jam
- Tomato Bruschetta Chicken
- Tomato Pesto Pasta
- Tomato and Burrata Salad
- Roasted Tomato Soup
- Tomato and Basil Frittata
- Tomato Chutney
- Tomato and Avocado Salsa
- Tomato Pie
- Tomato and Eggplant Parmesan
- Sun-Dried Tomato Pesto
- Tomato and Cucumber Salad
- Tomato and Spinach Quiche
- Tomato and Mozzarella Stuffed Chicken
- Tomato and Corn Salad
- Tomato and Lentil Soup
- Tomato and Onion Gratin
- Tomato and Feta Couscous
- Tomato and Pancetta Risotto
- Tomato and Basil Bruschetta
- Tomato and Garlic Shrimp
- Tomato and Herb Focaccia

- Tomato and Zucchini Tian
- Tomato and Artichoke Pizza
- Tomato and Pesto Crostini
- Tomato and Mushroom Risotto
- Tomato and Sausage Pasta
- Tomato and Olive Tapenade
- Tomato and Chickpea Stew
- Tomato and Herb Quinoa
- Tomato and Bacon Jam
- Tomato and Ricotta Gnocchi
- Tomato and Tuna Salad
- Tomato and Basil Pesto
- Tomato and Pepper Ratatouille
- Tomato and Herbed Rice Pilaf
- Tomato and Basil Bruschetta

Classic Marinara Sauce

Ingredients:

- 2 tablespoons olive oil
- 1 small onion, finely chopped
- 4 cloves garlic, minced
- 1/4 teaspoon red pepper flakes (optional, for heat)
- 1 (28-ounce) can crushed tomatoes
- 1 (14-ounce) can diced tomatoes
- 1 teaspoon dried oregano
- 1 teaspoon dried basil
- 1 teaspoon sugar (optional, to balance acidity)
- Salt and pepper, to taste
- Fresh basil leaves, chopped (for garnish, optional)

Instructions:

1. Sauté Aromatics:
    - In a large saucepan or Dutch oven, heat the olive oil over medium heat. Add the chopped onion and cook until softened and translucent, about 5-7 minutes.
2. Add Garlic and Red Pepper Flakes:
    - Add the minced garlic and red pepper flakes (if using) to the pan. Sauté for 1-2 minutes until fragrant, being careful not to burn the garlic.
3. Simmer Tomatoes:
    - Stir in the crushed tomatoes and diced tomatoes (including their juices) into the pan. Bring the mixture to a simmer.
4. Seasoning:
    - Add dried oregano, dried basil, and sugar (if using) to the sauce. Season with salt and pepper to taste. Stir well to combine.
5. Simmer:
    - Reduce the heat to low and let the marinara sauce simmer gently for 20-30 minutes, stirring occasionally. This helps develop the flavors and thicken the sauce.
6. Adjust Consistency (Optional):
    - If the sauce is too thick, you can add a little water or vegetable broth to reach your desired consistency. Simmer for a few more minutes after adjusting.
7. Finish:
    - Remove the marinara sauce from heat. Taste and adjust seasoning if needed. Stir in fresh chopped basil leaves for added freshness and flavor.
8. Serve:
    - Use the marinara sauce immediately over cooked pasta, as a dipping sauce for breadsticks, or as a base for pizza. Alternatively, let it cool completely before

storing in an airtight container in the refrigerator for up to 5 days or freeze for longer storage.

Tips:

- Fresh Tomatoes: If you prefer, you can substitute fresh tomatoes. Use about 2 pounds of ripe tomatoes, peeled and diced, in place of canned tomatoes.
- Variations: Customize your marinara sauce by adding other herbs like parsley or thyme, or a splash of red wine for extra depth of flavor.
- Versatility: Marinara sauce is incredibly versatile and can be used in a variety of dishes beyond pasta, such as chicken Parmesan, lasagna, or as a sauce for meatballs.

This classic marinara sauce recipe is simple yet full of robust tomato flavor, making it a perfect base for countless Italian-inspired dishes. Enjoy the homemade taste of this timeless sauce!

Caprese Salad

Ingredients:

- 2 large ripe tomatoes, sliced into 1/4-inch thick rounds
- 1 ball of fresh mozzarella cheese, sliced into 1/4-inch thick rounds
- Fresh basil leaves
- Extra virgin olive oil
- Balsamic glaze (optional, for drizzling)
- Salt and freshly ground black pepper, to taste

Instructions:

1. Prepare the Ingredients:
    - Wash and dry the tomatoes and basil leaves. Slice the tomatoes and fresh mozzarella cheese into rounds of equal thickness, about 1/4-inch thick.
2. Assemble the Salad:
    - Arrange the tomato slices and mozzarella slices alternately on a serving platter or individual plates. You can overlap them slightly for a visually appealing presentation.
3. Add Basil Leaves:
    - Place fresh basil leaves between the tomato and mozzarella slices. You can use whole leaves or tear them into smaller pieces.
4. Season:
    - Drizzle the Caprese salad with extra virgin olive oil. Use a good quality olive oil for the best flavor. Sprinkle with salt and freshly ground black pepper to taste.
5. Optional Garnish:
    - Optionally, drizzle balsamic glaze over the salad for a sweet and tangy finish. This is traditionally done by reducing balsamic vinegar until thickened, but store-bought balsamic glaze works well too.
6. Serve:
    - Serve the Caprese salad immediately as an appetizer or side dish. It's best enjoyed fresh when the flavors are vibrant.

Tips:

- Tomato Varieties: Use ripe, flavorful tomatoes such as heirloom tomatoes or vine-ripened tomatoes for the best taste.
- Mozzarella: Fresh mozzarella cheese is key to this salad. Look for it in the deli or cheese section of your grocery store.
- Presentation: Arrange the salad on a platter in a circular pattern for a classic look, or get creative with your presentation.

Caprese salad is a perfect dish for summer when tomatoes and basil are at their peak. It celebrates simple ingredients and showcases their natural flavors beautifully. Enjoy this refreshing and elegant salad as a starter or alongside grilled meats and crusty bread for a complete meal.

Margherita Pizza

Ingredients:

For the Pizza Dough:

- 1 pound (about 4 cups) pizza dough, homemade or store-bought
- Cornmeal or flour, for dusting

For the Toppings:

- 1/2 cup tomato sauce or marinara sauce
- 8 ounces fresh mozzarella cheese, sliced or torn into small pieces
- Fresh basil leaves, torn or chopped
- Extra virgin olive oil, for drizzling
- Salt and freshly ground black pepper, to taste

Instructions:

1. Preheat the Oven:
    - Preheat your oven to the highest temperature it can go, typically around 475°F to 500°F (245°C to 260°C). If you have a pizza stone, place it in the oven while preheating.
2. Prepare the Dough:
    - Dust a work surface with cornmeal or flour. Roll out the pizza dough into a circle or rectangle, about 12 inches in diameter or to your desired thickness. Transfer the rolled-out dough to a lightly floured pizza peel or parchment paper (if using a pizza stone) for easy transfer to the oven.
3. Add Sauce and Cheese:
    - Spread the tomato sauce evenly over the pizza dough, leaving a small border around the edges for the crust. Arrange the fresh mozzarella cheese pieces on top of the sauce.
4. Bake the Pizza:
    - Carefully slide the pizza onto the preheated pizza stone in the oven, if using. Alternatively, place the pizza on a baking sheet if you don't have a pizza stone.
    - Bake for 10-12 minutes, or until the crust is golden brown and the cheese is melted and bubbly.
5. Add Basil and Finish:
    - Remove the pizza from the oven. Sprinkle torn or chopped fresh basil leaves over the hot pizza.
    - Drizzle the Margherita pizza with extra virgin olive oil. Season with salt and freshly ground black pepper to taste.
6. Serve:
    - Slice the Margherita pizza and serve hot. Enjoy the fresh flavors of tomato, mozzarella, and basil in every bite!

Tips:

- Pizza Dough: For homemade dough, you can use a basic pizza dough recipe or buy pre-made dough from your local grocery store or pizzeria.
- Tomato Sauce: Use a good quality tomato sauce or marinara sauce. You can also make your own by simmering crushed tomatoes with garlic, olive oil, and herbs.
- Fresh Mozzarella: Opt for fresh mozzarella cheese for its creamy texture and mild flavor. It melts beautifully on the pizza.
- Basil: Fresh basil adds a burst of freshness to the pizza. Tear the basil leaves rather than chopping them to release their aroma.

Margherita pizza is a timeless favorite that highlights the simplicity and quality of its ingredients. Whether you're making it for a casual dinner or a special occasion, this pizza is sure to be a hit with its classic Italian flavors.

Tomato Basil Soup

Ingredients:

- 2 tablespoons olive oil
- 1 onion, chopped
- 3 cloves garlic, minced
- 2 (28-ounce) cans whole peeled tomatoes
- 1/2 cup fresh basil leaves, chopped (plus extra for garnish)
- 4 cups vegetable broth or chicken broth
- 1 teaspoon dried oregano
- 1 teaspoon dried thyme
- Salt and pepper, to taste
- 1/2 cup heavy cream (optional, for added creaminess)
- Grated Parmesan cheese, for serving (optional)
- Croutons or crusty bread, for serving (optional)

Instructions:

1. Sauté Aromatics:
    - In a large pot or Dutch oven, heat olive oil over medium heat. Add chopped onion and sauté until translucent, about 5-7 minutes. Add minced garlic and cook for another 1-2 minutes until fragrant.
2. Simmer Tomatoes:
    - Pour in the cans of whole peeled tomatoes with their juices. Use a wooden spoon to break up the tomatoes into smaller pieces. Stir in chopped basil leaves.
3. Add Broth and Seasonings:
    - Pour in the vegetable or chicken broth. Add dried oregano, dried thyme, salt, and pepper to taste. Bring the mixture to a boil, then reduce heat to low. Let it simmer uncovered for about 20-25 minutes, stirring occasionally.
4. Blend the Soup:
    - Remove the soup from heat. Using an immersion blender directly in the pot, blend the soup until smooth. Alternatively, carefully transfer the soup in batches to a blender and blend until smooth. Be cautious as hot liquids can splatter.
5. Optional Cream (for added richness):
    - Stir in heavy cream, if using, to add richness to the soup. Adjust seasoning with salt and pepper if needed.
6. Serve:
    - Ladle the tomato basil soup into bowls. Garnish with additional chopped basil leaves, grated Parmesan cheese, and a drizzle of olive oil if desired. Serve with croutons or crusty bread on the side.

Tips:

- **Tomatoes:** Use good quality canned whole peeled tomatoes for the best flavor. San Marzano tomatoes are a popular choice.
- **Fresh Basil:** Fresh basil adds a wonderful aroma and flavor to the soup. If you don't have fresh basil, you can use dried basil, but adjust the quantity as dried herbs are more potent.
- **Creamy Texture:** For a dairy-free option, you can omit the heavy cream or use coconut milk for a creamy texture.
- **Storage:** Tomato basil soup can be stored in an airtight container in the refrigerator for up to 4 days. Reheat gently on the stove before serving.

This tomato basil soup recipe is perfect for any time of year, providing warmth and comfort with its rich tomato flavor and aromatic basil. Enjoy this soup as a starter or light meal, paired with your favorite bread for dipping!

Bruschetta

Ingredients:

- 1 French baguette or Italian bread, sliced into 1/2-inch thick slices
- 4-5 ripe tomatoes, diced
- 2 cloves garlic, minced
- 1/4 cup fresh basil leaves, chopped
- 2 tablespoons extra virgin olive oil, plus extra for drizzling
- 1 teaspoon balsamic vinegar (optional)
- Salt and freshly ground black pepper, to taste

Instructions:

1. Toast the Bread:
   - Preheat your oven to 400°F (200°C). Arrange the bread slices on a baking sheet in a single layer. Drizzle or brush each slice lightly with olive oil. Bake for about 8-10 minutes, or until the bread is crispy and lightly golden. You can also toast the bread on a grill or in a toaster.
2. Prepare the Topping:
   - In a mixing bowl, combine the diced tomatoes, minced garlic, chopped basil leaves, olive oil, and balsamic vinegar (if using). Season with salt and freshly ground black pepper to taste. Mix well to combine.
3. Assemble the Bruschetta:
   - Once the bread slices are toasted and cooled slightly, spoon the tomato mixture generously onto each slice of bread. Ensure each slice gets a good amount of tomatoes and juices.
4. Serve:
   - Arrange the bruschetta on a serving platter. Drizzle a little extra virgin olive oil over the top for added flavor and presentation. Garnish with additional fresh basil leaves if desired.
5. Optional Variations:
   - Add a slice of fresh mozzarella cheese on top of each bruschetta slice before adding the tomato mixture for a creamy variation.
   - Top with a sprinkle of grated Parmesan cheese for added richness.

Tips:

- Tomatoes: Use ripe and flavorful tomatoes, such as Roma or vine-ripened tomatoes, for the best taste.
- Bread: Choose a good quality French baguette or Italian bread that will hold up to toasting and topping without becoming too soggy.
- Make-Ahead: You can prepare the tomato topping ahead of time and store it in the refrigerator. Toast the bread slices just before serving to ensure they stay crispy.

Bruschetta is a versatile dish that makes a delicious appetizer for parties or a light and refreshing snack. It's best enjoyed fresh, allowing the flavors of the tomatoes, garlic, basil, and olive oil to meld together. Enjoy the taste of Italy with this simple and flavorful bruschetta recipe!

Stuffed Tomatoes

Ingredients:

- 6 large tomatoes
- 1 cup cooked rice (white or brown)
- 1/2 cup grated Parmesan cheese
- 1/4 cup breadcrumbs
- 1/4 cup chopped fresh herbs (such as parsley, basil, or thyme)
- 2 cloves garlic, minced
- 2 tablespoons olive oil
- Salt and pepper, to taste
- Optional: 1/4 cup chopped onions or bell peppers for added flavor

Instructions:

1. Prepare the Tomatoes:
   - Preheat your oven to 375°F (190°C). Grease a baking dish lightly with olive oil or cooking spray.
   - Wash the tomatoes and cut off the tops. Using a spoon, carefully scoop out the flesh and seeds from the center of each tomato, leaving a sturdy shell. Reserve the flesh and juices in a bowl.
2. Prepare the Filling:
   - In a mixing bowl, combine the cooked rice, grated Parmesan cheese, breadcrumbs, chopped fresh herbs, minced garlic, olive oil, and optional chopped onions or bell peppers. Mix well to combine.
3. Season and Fill the Tomatoes:
   - Season the tomato shells with salt and pepper. Spoon the filling mixture evenly into each tomato shell, pressing gently to pack it in.
4. Bake the Stuffed Tomatoes:
   - Place the stuffed tomatoes in the prepared baking dish. If there is any leftover filling, you can sprinkle it around the tomatoes in the dish.
   - Bake in the preheated oven for 25-30 minutes, or until the tomatoes are tender and the tops are golden brown.
5. Serve:
   - Remove the stuffed tomatoes from the oven and let them cool slightly before serving. Garnish with additional fresh herbs if desired.

Tips:

- Variations: You can customize the filling based on your preferences. Consider adding cooked ground meat, quinoa, couscous, or other grains instead of rice. You can also vary the cheese or herbs used.

- Presentation: Serve stuffed tomatoes as a side dish with grilled meats or fish, or as an appetizer at parties.
- Make-Ahead: You can prepare the stuffing mixture and hollow out the tomatoes in advance. Keep them refrigerated separately, then assemble and bake just before serving.

Stuffed tomatoes are a delicious way to enjoy fresh produce and can be adapted to suit different dietary preferences. Experiment with different fillings and enjoy this versatile dish as part of your next meal!

Tomato Risotto

Ingredients:

- 1 tablespoon olive oil
- 1 tablespoon butter
- 1 onion, finely chopped
- 2 cloves garlic, minced
- 1 1/2 cups Arborio rice
- 1/2 cup dry white wine (optional)
- 4 cups vegetable or chicken broth, heated and kept warm
- 1 cup diced tomatoes (fresh or canned)
- 1/2 cup grated Parmesan cheese
- 2 tablespoons tomato paste
- 1 tablespoon chopped fresh basil
- Salt and pepper, to taste

Instructions:

1. Prepare Ingredients:
    - Heat the vegetable or chicken broth in a saucepan and keep it warm over low heat.
2. Sauté Aromatics:
    - In a large, heavy-bottomed pot or Dutch oven, heat the olive oil and butter over medium heat. Add the chopped onion and sauté until softened and translucent, about 5-7 minutes. Add the minced garlic and cook for another 1-2 minutes until fragrant.
3. Toast the Rice:
    - Add the Arborio rice to the pot with the onions and garlic. Stir well to coat the rice in the oil and butter mixture. Cook for 1-2 minutes, stirring constantly, until the rice becomes slightly translucent.
4. Deglaze with Wine (optional):
    - If using wine, pour the white wine into the pot and stir continuously until the wine is absorbed by the rice.
5. Add Tomatoes:
    - Stir in the diced tomatoes and tomato paste. Cook for another minute to combine flavors.
6. Cook the Risotto:
    - Begin adding the warm broth to the rice mixture, one ladleful (about 1/2 cup) at a time. Stir frequently and allow each addition of broth to be absorbed before adding more. This process will take about 18-20 minutes, and the rice should be creamy but still slightly al dente.
7. Finish the Risotto:

- Once the rice is cooked to your desired consistency, remove the pot from heat. Stir in the grated Parmesan cheese and chopped fresh basil. Season with salt and pepper to taste.
8. Serve:
    - Serve the tomato risotto immediately, garnished with additional grated Parmesan cheese and fresh basil leaves if desired.

Tips:

- Tomatoes: Use ripe and flavorful tomatoes for the best taste. Fresh diced tomatoes work well, but you can also use canned diced tomatoes if fresh are not available.
- Broth: Warm broth is crucial for cooking risotto evenly and achieving a creamy texture. Use vegetable broth for a vegetarian version or chicken broth for added depth of flavor.
- Consistency: Risotto should have a creamy consistency with each grain of rice distinct but tender. Adjust the amount of broth and cooking time as needed to achieve this.

Tomato risotto makes for a satisfying main dish or a delightful side, perfect for showcasing the flavors of ripe tomatoes and creamy Arborio rice. Enjoy this comforting Italian dish as a hearty meal!

Tomato and Mozzarella Panini

Ingredients:

- 4 slices of ciabatta bread or your favorite sandwich bread
- 2 medium-sized tomatoes, thinly sliced
- 8 ounces fresh mozzarella cheese, sliced
- Fresh basil leaves
- Olive oil or butter, for grilling
- Salt and pepper, to taste

Instructions:

1. Preheat the Panini Press:
   - Preheat your panini press according to the manufacturer's instructions. If you don't have a panini press, you can use a grill pan or a regular skillet.
2. Assemble the Sandwich:
   - Take two slices of ciabatta bread and layer each with slices of mozzarella cheese, followed by tomato slices. Season the tomatoes with a pinch of salt and pepper. Add fresh basil leaves on top.
3. Close the Sandwich:
   - Place the remaining two slices of ciabatta bread on top of each sandwich to close them.
4. Grill the Panini:
   - Brush the outside of each sandwich with olive oil or spread butter lightly on each side. Place the sandwiches on the preheated panini press or grill pan.
5. Press and Grill:
   - Close the panini press or grill pan and press down gently. If using a grill pan or skillet, press the sandwiches down with a spatula. Cook for 4-5 minutes, or until the bread is golden brown and the cheese is melted.
6. Serve:
   - Remove the Tomato and Mozzarella Panini from the panini press or grill pan. Let them cool for a minute, then slice in half diagonally. Serve hot and enjoy!

Tips:

- Bread: Ciabatta bread works well for paninis due to its sturdy texture, but you can use any sandwich bread you prefer.
- Cheese: Fresh mozzarella cheese is ideal for its creamy texture when melted. You can also use shredded mozzarella or other melting cheeses like provolone or fontina.
- Variations: Add a drizzle of balsamic glaze or pesto sauce for extra flavor. You can also add thinly sliced prosciutto or grilled chicken for a heartier panini.

Tomato and Mozzarella Panini is a versatile and flavorful sandwich that's perfect for a quick lunch or dinner. Enjoy the combination of melty cheese, juicy tomatoes, and aromatic basil in every bite!

Gazpacho

Ingredients:

- 6 ripe tomatoes, chopped
- 1 cucumber, peeled, seeded, and chopped
- 1 red bell pepper, seeded and chopped
- 1 small red onion, chopped
- 2 cloves garlic, minced
- 3 cups tomato juice
- 1/4 cup extra virgin olive oil
- 2 tablespoons red wine vinegar
- 1 tablespoon fresh lemon juice
- 1 teaspoon salt, or to taste
- 1/2 teaspoon black pepper, or to taste
- Optional garnishes: chopped fresh herbs (such as basil or parsley), croutons, diced cucumber, chopped bell pepper

Instructions:

1. Prepare the Vegetables:
   - Wash and chop all the vegetables as specified.
2. Blend the Soup:
   - In a blender or food processor, combine the chopped tomatoes, cucumber, red bell pepper, red onion, and garlic. Blend until smooth or your desired consistency. You may need to work in batches depending on the size of your blender.
3. Combine Ingredients:
   - Transfer the blended vegetables to a large bowl. Stir in the tomato juice, olive oil, red wine vinegar, and lemon juice. Mix well to combine.
4. Season:
   - Season the gazpacho with salt and black pepper to taste. Adjust the seasoning as needed.
5. Chill:
   - Cover the bowl with plastic wrap or a lid and refrigerate the gazpacho for at least 2 hours, or until thoroughly chilled. Chilling allows the flavors to meld together.
6. Serve:
   - Stir the gazpacho well before serving. Ladle into bowls and garnish with your choice of optional garnishes, such as chopped fresh herbs, croutons, diced cucumber, or chopped bell pepper.

Tips:

- Texture: Gazpacho can be blended until completely smooth or left slightly chunky, depending on your preference.

- Make-Ahead: Gazpacho tastes even better the next day as the flavors continue to develop. Store it in the refrigerator in an airtight container for up to 3 days.
- Variations: Some variations include adding a small amount of hot sauce for a spicy kick or blending in a piece of stale bread to thicken the soup.

Gazpacho is a versatile dish that can be served as an appetizer or light meal. It's known for its vibrant color and refreshing taste, making it a perfect dish to enjoy during the summer months. Serve it chilled and savor the fresh flavors of ripe tomatoes and vegetables!

Ratatouille

Ingredients:

- 1 large eggplant, diced into 1-inch cubes
- 2 medium zucchinis, diced
- 1 large red bell pepper, diced
- 1 large yellow bell pepper, diced
- 1 large onion, diced
- 4 cloves garlic, minced
- 4 ripe tomatoes, diced (or 1 can of diced tomatoes)
- 2 tablespoons tomato paste
- 2 tablespoons olive oil
- 1 teaspoon dried thyme
- 1 teaspoon dried oregano
- 1/2 teaspoon dried basil
- Salt and pepper, to taste
- Fresh basil or parsley, chopped, for garnish

Instructions:

1. Prepare the Vegetables:
    - Heat 1 tablespoon of olive oil in a large skillet or Dutch oven over medium-high heat. Add the diced eggplant and cook until lightly browned and softened, about 5-7 minutes. Remove from the skillet and set aside.
2. Cook the Onions and Peppers:
    - In the same skillet, add the remaining tablespoon of olive oil. Add the diced onion, red bell pepper, and yellow bell pepper. Sauté until softened, about 5 minutes.
3. Combine Ingredients:
    - Stir in the minced garlic and cook for another 1-2 minutes until fragrant. Add the diced tomatoes, tomato paste, dried thyme, dried oregano, dried basil, salt, and pepper. Mix well to combine.
4. Simmer the Ratatouille:
    - Reduce the heat to medium-low and let the mixture simmer for 10-15 minutes, stirring occasionally, until the vegetables are tender and the flavors have melded together.
5. Add Zucchini and Eggplant:
    - Add the diced zucchini and cooked eggplant back into the skillet. Stir gently to combine with the other vegetables. Cook for an additional 5-7 minutes, or until the zucchini is tender but still retains its shape.
6. Adjust Seasoning:
    - Taste and adjust seasoning with salt and pepper if needed.
7. Serve:

- Remove the ratatouille from heat. Serve hot, garnished with chopped fresh basil or parsley.

Tips:

- Vegetable Prep: Cut the vegetables into uniform pieces for even cooking.
- Variations: Ratatouille is versatile and can be served as a side dish, over pasta or rice, or even as a topping for crusty bread. Some variations include adding fresh herbs like rosemary or thyme, or a splash of balsamic vinegar for extra flavor.
- Storage: Ratatouille tastes even better the next day as the flavors develop. Store it in the refrigerator in an airtight container for up to 4 days. Reheat gently on the stove before serving.

Ratatouille is a hearty and satisfying dish that celebrates the flavors of summer vegetables. Enjoy this classic French stew as a vegetarian main course or a flavorful side dish!

Tomato Confit

Ingredients:

- 2 pounds ripe tomatoes (plum or Roma tomatoes work well)
- 4-5 cloves garlic, peeled and smashed
- 1/2 cup extra virgin olive oil
- 1 teaspoon dried thyme (or a few sprigs of fresh thyme)
- 1 teaspoon dried oregano
- Salt and freshly ground black pepper, to taste
- Optional: red pepper flakes for a bit of heat
- Fresh basil or parsley, chopped, for garnish

Instructions:

1. Preheat the Oven:
    - Preheat your oven to 300°F (150°C).
2. Prepare the Tomatoes:
    - Wash the tomatoes and cut them in half lengthwise. If using larger tomatoes, you can quarter them. Remove the core and seeds if desired, but it's not necessary.
3. Combine Ingredients:
    - In a baking dish or oven-safe skillet, arrange the tomato halves cut-side up. Scatter the smashed garlic cloves over the tomatoes.
4. Season and Drizzle:
    - Drizzle the extra virgin olive oil evenly over the tomatoes and garlic. Sprinkle with dried thyme, dried oregano, salt, and freshly ground black pepper. Add a pinch of red pepper flakes if desired for some heat.
5. Bake the Tomato Confit:
    - Place the baking dish or skillet in the preheated oven. Bake for 1.5 to 2 hours, or until the tomatoes are very tender and caramelized, and the edges start to brown slightly. The cooking time may vary depending on the size and juiciness of your tomatoes.
6. Cool and Serve:
    - Remove the tomato confit from the oven and let it cool slightly. Garnish with chopped fresh basil or parsley before serving.
7. Storage:
    - Tomato confit can be stored in an airtight container in the refrigerator for up to one week. It can also be frozen for longer storage.

Serving Suggestions:

- As a Spread: Serve tomato confit as a spread on crusty bread or toast. It's delicious on its own or with a sprinkle of goat cheese or feta.

- With Pasta: Toss tomato confit with cooked pasta and a drizzle of olive oil for a simple yet flavorful pasta dish.
- On Salads: Use tomato confit to enhance salads, sandwiches, or as a topping for grilled meats or fish.

Tomato confit is versatile and adds a burst of rich tomato flavor to a variety of dishes. Enjoy its sweet and savory taste as a condiment, side dish, or ingredient in your favorite recipes!

Tomato Tart

Ingredients:

For the Tart Crust:

- 1 1/4 cups all-purpose flour
- 1/2 teaspoon salt
- 1/2 cup unsalted butter, chilled and diced
- 3-4 tablespoons ice water

For the Filling:

- 3-4 ripe tomatoes, sliced (about 1/4-inch thick)
- 1 cup shredded cheese (such as Gruyère, mozzarella, or goat cheese)
- 1/4 cup fresh basil leaves, chopped
- 2 tablespoons Dijon mustard (optional, for spreading on the crust)
- Salt and pepper, to taste
- Olive oil, for drizzling
- Optional: balsamic glaze or reduction for drizzling after baking

Instructions:

1. Prepare the Tart Crust:
    - In a food processor, pulse together the flour and salt. Add the chilled butter and pulse until the mixture resembles coarse crumbs.
    - Gradually add the ice water, 1 tablespoon at a time, and pulse until the dough comes together. You may not need all of the water.
    - Turn the dough out onto a lightly floured surface and gather it into a ball. Flatten into a disk, wrap in plastic wrap, and refrigerate for at least 30 minutes.
2. Preheat the Oven:
    - Preheat your oven to 375°F (190°C).
3. Roll Out the Dough:
    - On a lightly floured surface, roll out the chilled dough into a circle or rectangle, about 1/8-inch thick. Transfer the rolled-out dough to a parchment-lined baking sheet.
4. Assemble the Tart:
    - If using, spread a thin layer of Dijon mustard evenly over the tart crust (optional but adds a nice flavor). Sprinkle half of the shredded cheese over the mustard (if using).
    - Arrange the tomato slices in a single layer over the cheese. Season the tomatoes with salt and pepper. Sprinkle the chopped basil over the tomatoes.
    - Sprinkle the remaining shredded cheese evenly over the tomatoes.
5. Bake the Tart:

- Drizzle olive oil over the assembled tart. Fold the edges of the dough over the filling, creating a rustic crust. You can brush the crust with an egg wash (1 egg beaten with 1 tablespoon of water) for a shiny finish if desired.
- Bake in the preheated oven for 30-35 minutes, or until the crust is golden brown and the tomatoes are tender.

6. Serve:
    - Remove the tomato tart from the oven and let it cool for a few minutes before slicing. Optionally, drizzle with balsamic glaze or reduction before serving.

Tips:

- Tomatoes: Use ripe tomatoes for the best flavor. You can use a variety of tomatoes such as heirloom or cherry tomatoes for different textures and colors.
- Cheese: Experiment with different cheeses to complement the tomatoes. Gruyère, mozzarella, and goat cheese all work well.
- Variations: Add caramelized onions, garlic, or fresh herbs like thyme or rosemary to customize the flavors of your tomato tart.

This tomato tart is perfect served warm or at room temperature, making it a versatile dish for brunch, lunch, or a light dinner. Enjoy the combination of flaky crust, juicy tomatoes, and creamy cheese in every bite!

Tomato and Goat Cheese Galette

Ingredients:

For the Galette Dough:

- 1 1/4 cups all-purpose flour
- 1/4 teaspoon salt
- 1/2 cup unsalted butter, chilled and cut into small pieces
- 1/4 cup ice water

For the Filling:

- 3-4 ripe tomatoes, thinly sliced (about 1/4-inch thick)
- 4 ounces goat cheese, crumbled
- 1 tablespoon fresh thyme leaves (or 1 teaspoon dried thyme)
- 1 tablespoon olive oil
- Salt and pepper, to taste
- Optional: 1 egg beaten with 1 tablespoon of water (for egg wash)
- Optional: balsamic glaze or reduction, for drizzling after baking

Instructions:

1. Prepare the Galette Dough:
    - In a food processor, pulse together the flour and salt. Add the chilled butter and pulse until the mixture resembles coarse crumbs.
    - Gradually add the ice water, 1 tablespoon at a time, pulsing until the dough just comes together.
    - Turn the dough out onto a lightly floured surface, gather it into a ball, flatten into a disk, wrap in plastic wrap, and refrigerate for at least 30 minutes.
2. Preheat the Oven:
    - Preheat your oven to 375°F (190°C). Line a baking sheet with parchment paper.
3. Roll Out the Dough:
    - On a lightly floured surface, roll out the chilled dough into a circle or rectangle, about 1/8-inch thick. Transfer the rolled-out dough to the prepared baking sheet.
4. Assemble the Galette:
    - Leaving a 1-2 inch border, sprinkle half of the crumbled goat cheese evenly over the dough.
    - Arrange the tomato slices in overlapping layers over the goat cheese, leaving the border intact. Sprinkle the thyme leaves over the tomatoes.
    - Drizzle olive oil over the tomatoes and season with salt and pepper.
5. Fold the Edges:
    - Fold the edges of the dough over the tomatoes, pleating as you go to create a rustic border. Press gently to seal the edges.
6. Optional Egg Wash:

- Brush the edges of the galette with the beaten egg wash for a golden finish.
7. Bake the Galette:
    - Bake in the preheated oven for 30-35 minutes, or until the crust is golden brown and crisp.
8. Serve:
    - Remove the galette from the oven and let it cool for a few minutes before slicing. Drizzle with balsamic glaze or reduction if desired before serving.

Tips:

- Tomatoes: Use ripe tomatoes for the best flavor. Roma or heirloom tomatoes work well.
- Goat Cheese: The tangy flavor of goat cheese complements the sweetness of tomatoes perfectly, but you can also use other cheeses like feta or mozzarella.
- Variations: Add caramelized onions, garlic, or fresh herbs like basil or rosemary to enhance the flavors of your galette.

This Tomato and Goat Cheese Galette is delicious served warm or at room temperature. It makes a fantastic appetizer, side dish, or light main course, perfect for showcasing the flavors of summer tomatoes and creamy goat cheese in a rustic pastry crust. Enjoy!

Tomato Jam

Ingredients:

- 2 pounds ripe tomatoes, peeled, seeded, and chopped
- 1 cup granulated sugar
- 1/4 cup packed brown sugar
- 1/4 cup apple cider vinegar
- 1 teaspoon ground ginger
- 1/2 teaspoon ground cinnamon
- 1/4 teaspoon ground cloves
- 1/4 teaspoon ground nutmeg
- Pinch of salt
- Zest and juice of 1 lemon

Instructions:

1. Prepare the Tomatoes:
    - To peel the tomatoes, score an "X" at the bottom of each tomato. Place them in boiling water for about 30 seconds, then transfer to an ice bath. Peel off the skins, remove the seeds, and chop the tomatoes.
2. Cook the Jam:
    - In a large, heavy-bottomed saucepan, combine the chopped tomatoes, granulated sugar, brown sugar, apple cider vinegar, ground ginger, ground cinnamon, ground cloves, ground nutmeg, and a pinch of salt.
    - Stir to combine and bring the mixture to a boil over medium-high heat.
3. Simmer:
    - Reduce the heat to medium-low and simmer the mixture, stirring occasionally, until it thickens to a jam-like consistency. This will take about 1 to 1.5 hours. As it cooks, mash the tomatoes with the back of a spoon or a potato masher to break them down.
4. Add Lemon:
    - Stir in the lemon zest and juice during the last 10 minutes of cooking.
5. Test for Doneness:
    - To test if the jam is ready, place a small amount on a chilled plate. If it holds its shape without being too runny, it's done.
6. Cool and Store:
    - Remove the pan from heat and let the tomato jam cool slightly. Transfer it to clean, sterilized jars or containers. Allow the jam to cool completely before sealing with lids.
7. Store and Serve:
    - Tomato jam can be stored in the refrigerator for up to 2 weeks. For longer storage, process the jars in a water bath for 10 minutes to seal them properly, then store in a cool, dark place for up to 6 months.

Serving Suggestions:

- Spread tomato jam on toasted bread or crostini, topped with goat cheese or cream cheese.
- Use it as a glaze for roasted meats such as chicken or pork.
- Serve alongside grilled cheese sandwiches or as a condiment for burgers.

Tomato jam adds a burst of sweet and savory flavor to a variety of dishes, making it a versatile and delicious addition to your pantry!

Tomato Bruschetta Chicken

Ingredients:

- 4 boneless, skinless chicken breasts
- Salt and pepper, to taste
- 2 tablespoons olive oil

For the Tomato Bruschetta:

- 4-5 ripe tomatoes, diced
- 2 cloves garlic, minced
- 1/4 cup fresh basil leaves, chopped
- 1 tablespoon balsamic vinegar
- 1 tablespoon extra virgin olive oil
- Salt and pepper, to taste
- Optional: 1/4 cup shredded mozzarella cheese or grated Parmesan cheese

Instructions:

1. Prepare the Tomato Bruschetta:
   - In a medium bowl, combine the diced tomatoes, minced garlic, chopped basil, balsamic vinegar, extra virgin olive oil, salt, and pepper. Mix well to combine. Set aside to marinate while you prepare the chicken.
2. Cook the Chicken:
   - Season both sides of the chicken breasts with salt and pepper.
   - In a large skillet, heat 2 tablespoons of olive oil over medium-high heat.
   - Add the chicken breasts to the skillet and cook for about 5-6 minutes on each side, or until they are golden brown and cooked through (internal temperature should reach 165°F or 74°C).
   - Remove the chicken breasts from the skillet and set aside.
3. Assemble the Dish:
   - Preheat your broiler (grill) on high.
   - Place the cooked chicken breasts on a baking sheet lined with foil or parchment paper.
   - Spoon the tomato bruschetta mixture generously over each chicken breast.
   - If desired, sprinkle shredded mozzarella or grated Parmesan cheese over the top of each chicken breast.
4. Broil (Grill):
   - Place the baking sheet under the broiler (grill) for 2-3 minutes, or until the cheese is melted and bubbly.
   - Keep a close eye on it to prevent burning.
5. Serve:
   - Remove from the oven and garnish with additional chopped basil if desired.

- Serve the Tomato Bruschetta Chicken hot, with a side of salad, rice, pasta, or crusty bread.

Tips:

- Tomato Mixture: Allow the tomato bruschetta mixture to marinate for at least 15-20 minutes before serving to enhance the flavors.
- Cheese: The addition of mozzarella or Parmesan cheese is optional but adds a delicious cheesy layer to the dish.
- Variations: You can also grill or bake the chicken breasts instead of pan-searing them. Adjust cooking times accordingly.

This Tomato Bruschetta Chicken recipe is simple yet flavorful, combining the freshness of tomatoes and basil with tender chicken. It's a perfect dish for a family dinner or when you want to impress guests with minimal effort. Enjoy!

Tomato Pesto Pasta

Ingredients:

- 12 ounces (340g) pasta of your choice (spaghetti, penne, or fusilli work well)
- 2 cups cherry tomatoes, halved (or use diced tomatoes)
- 2 cloves garlic, minced
- 1/4 cup basil pesto (store-bought or homemade)
- 1/4 cup grated Parmesan cheese
- Salt and freshly ground black pepper, to taste
- Fresh basil leaves, chopped, for garnish (optional)
- Extra virgin olive oil, for drizzling

Instructions:

1. Cook the Pasta:
    - Bring a large pot of salted water to a boil. Cook the pasta according to the package instructions until al dente. Reserve about 1/2 cup of pasta cooking water, then drain the pasta.
2. Prepare the Sauce:
    - In a large skillet or saucepan, heat a drizzle of olive oil over medium heat. Add the minced garlic and cook for about 1 minute, until fragrant.
    - Add the halved cherry tomatoes to the skillet. Cook for 3-4 minutes, stirring occasionally, until the tomatoes start to soften and release their juices.
3. Combine Pasta and Sauce:
    - Add the cooked pasta to the skillet with the tomatoes and garlic. Toss to combine.
4. Add Pesto:
    - Stir in the basil pesto until the pasta is well coated. If the pasta seems dry, add some of the reserved pasta cooking water a little at a time to loosen the sauce.
5. Season and Serve:
    - Stir in grated Parmesan cheese. Season with salt and pepper to taste.
6. Garnish and Serve:
    - Remove from heat and garnish with chopped fresh basil leaves, if desired. Drizzle with a bit of extra virgin olive oil before serving.

Tips:

- Tomatoes: You can use cherry tomatoes, grape tomatoes, or diced fresh tomatoes. Cooking them briefly in the skillet allows their flavors to concentrate.
- Pesto: Use store-bought basil pesto for convenience, or make your own for a fresher flavor. Adjust the amount of pesto to suit your taste.
- Cheese: Parmesan cheese adds a salty and nutty flavor. You can also use pecorino Romano or another hard cheese.

This tomato pesto pasta is quick to make and bursting with flavors from the fresh tomatoes and basil pesto. It's perfect for a satisfying weeknight meal or a quick lunch. Enjoy this delicious pasta dish!

Tomato and Burrata Salad

Ingredients:

- 4-5 ripe tomatoes, sliced (use a variety like heirloom tomatoes for color and flavor)
- 1 ball of burrata cheese (about 8 ounces)
- Fresh basil leaves, torn or chopped
- Extra virgin olive oil, for drizzling
- Balsamic glaze or reduction, for drizzling (optional)
- Salt and freshly ground black pepper, to taste

Instructions:

1. Prepare the Tomatoes:
    - Wash and dry the tomatoes. Slice them into 1/4-inch thick rounds or wedges, depending on your preference.
2. Assemble the Salad:
    - Arrange the sliced tomatoes on a serving platter or individual plates.
3. Prepare the Burrata:
    - Carefully cut or tear the burrata cheese into pieces and place them over the tomatoes.
4. Season and Garnish:
    - Sprinkle the torn or chopped basil leaves over the tomatoes and burrata.
    - Drizzle extra virgin olive oil generously over the salad.
5. Season and Serve:
    - Season with salt and freshly ground black pepper to taste.
    - Optionally, drizzle with balsamic glaze or reduction for extra sweetness and flavor.
6. Serve Immediately:
    - Serve the Tomato and Burrata Salad immediately as an appetizer or a side dish.

Tips:

- Tomatoes: Use a variety of tomatoes for different colors and flavors. Heirloom tomatoes are particularly flavorful.
- Burrata Cheese: Burrata is a fresh Italian cheese known for its creamy center. It adds richness to the salad. If you can't find burrata, you can substitute with fresh mozzarella or buffalo mozzarella.
- Basil: Fresh basil complements the tomatoes and cheese beautifully. Tear or chop the basil just before serving to retain its freshness.
- Drizzles: A good quality extra virgin olive oil and balsamic glaze elevate the flavors of this simple salad.

This Tomato and Burrata Salad is a perfect representation of summer with its vibrant colors and fresh flavors. It's quick to prepare and makes an elegant and delicious addition to any meal. Enjoy this salad as a light lunch or starter!

Roasted Tomato Soup

Ingredients:

- 2 pounds ripe tomatoes, halved (Roma or plum tomatoes work well)
- 1 onion, peeled and quartered
- 4 cloves garlic, peeled
- 2 tablespoons olive oil
- Salt and freshly ground black pepper, to taste
- 1 teaspoon dried thyme (or 2-3 sprigs of fresh thyme)
- 4 cups vegetable broth or chicken broth
- 1/2 cup heavy cream (optional, for a creamy soup)
- Fresh basil leaves, chopped, for garnish
- Croutons or crusty bread, for serving (optional)

Instructions:

1. Preheat the Oven:
    - Preheat your oven to 400°F (200°C).
2. Prepare the Tomatoes and Vegetables:
    - Place the halved tomatoes, quartered onion, and peeled garlic cloves on a baking sheet lined with parchment paper.
    - Drizzle with olive oil and season with salt, pepper, and dried thyme.
3. Roast the Vegetables:
    - Roast in the preheated oven for 40-45 minutes, or until the tomatoes are soft and caramelized.
4. Blend the Soup:
    - Once roasted, transfer the tomatoes, onion, and garlic to a blender or food processor (you may need to do this in batches depending on the size of your blender).
    - Add 2 cups of vegetable or chicken broth to the blender and blend until smooth. Adjust the consistency by adding more broth as needed.
5. Heat the Soup:
    - Pour the blended mixture into a large pot or saucepan. Stir in the remaining 2 cups of broth.
    - Bring the soup to a simmer over medium heat. If using, stir in the heavy cream for a creamy texture (optional).
    - Taste and adjust seasoning with salt and pepper if needed.
6. Serve:
    - Ladle the roasted tomato soup into bowls. Garnish with chopped fresh basil leaves.
    - Serve hot, optionally with croutons or crusty bread on the side.

Tips:

- Tomatoes: Use ripe, flavorful tomatoes for the best results. Roasting enhances their natural sweetness and depth of flavor.
- Vegetables: Roasting the onion and garlic alongside the tomatoes adds complexity to the soup.
- Cream: Adding heavy cream is optional but creates a richer and creamier soup. You can omit it for a lighter version.
- Garnish: Fresh basil adds a bright, herbaceous note to the soup. You can also drizzle with a swirl of olive oil before serving.

This roasted tomato soup is comforting and perfect for cooler days. It's a versatile dish that can be enjoyed as a starter or as a light meal with bread on the side. Enjoy the rich flavors of roasted tomatoes in this simple and satisfying soup!

Tomato and Basil Frittata

Ingredients:

- 6 large eggs
- 1/4 cup milk or cream
- 1 cup cherry tomatoes, halved
- 1/2 cup fresh basil leaves, chopped
- 1/2 cup grated Parmesan cheese
- Salt and pepper, to taste
- Olive oil

Instructions:

1. Preheat your oven: Start by preheating your oven to 350°F (175°C).
2. Prepare the eggs: Crack the eggs into a bowl and whisk them together with the milk or cream until well combined. Season with salt and pepper to taste.
3. Prepare the tomatoes and basil: Wash and halve the cherry tomatoes. Chop the fresh basil leaves.
4. Cooking the frittata:
    - Heat an oven-safe skillet over medium heat and add a drizzle of olive oil.
    - Once the oil is hot, add the cherry tomatoes to the skillet and sauté for about 2-3 minutes until they start to soften.
    - Pour the egg mixture evenly over the tomatoes in the skillet.
    - Sprinkle the chopped basil evenly over the eggs.
    - Cook the frittata on the stove for about 3-4 minutes until the edges start to set.
5. Bake the frittata: Sprinkle the grated Parmesan cheese evenly over the top of the frittata. Transfer the skillet to the preheated oven and bake for 10-12 minutes, or until the frittata is set in the center and the top is lightly golden.
6. Serve: Once cooked through, remove the skillet from the oven (remember to use an oven mitt, as the handle will be hot). Let it cool slightly, then slice and serve warm.

Tips:

- You can customize this frittata by adding other ingredients like sautéed onions, bell peppers, spinach, or different cheeses.
- Make sure to use an oven-safe skillet since the frittata will be transferred from stovetop to oven.
- For a dairy-free option, you can omit the cheese or use a dairy-free alternative.

Enjoy your Tomato and Basil Frittata as a flavorful and satisfying meal!

Tomato Chutney

Ingredients:

- 4 medium-sized tomatoes, chopped
- 1 medium onion, chopped
- 2-3 cloves of garlic, minced
- 1-inch piece of ginger, minced
- 2-3 dried red chilies (adjust to taste)
- 1/2 teaspoon mustard seeds
- 1/2 teaspoon cumin seeds
- 1/4 teaspoon fenugreek seeds (optional)
- 1/2 teaspoon turmeric powder
- 1/2 teaspoon red chili powder (adjust to taste)
- 1 tablespoon vegetable oil
- Salt to taste
- 1-2 tablespoons sugar or jaggery (adjust to balance acidity)
- 1 tablespoon vinegar or lemon juice (optional, for tanginess)

Instructions:

1. Prepare the tomatoes: Chop the tomatoes into medium-sized pieces. Also, chop the onion, garlic, and ginger.
2. Tempering spices: Heat oil in a pan over medium heat. Add mustard seeds and let them splutter. Add cumin seeds and fenugreek seeds (if using), and sauté for a few seconds until fragrant.
3. Sauté aromatics: Add minced garlic, ginger, and dried red chilies. Sauté for a minute until garlic turns golden brown.
4. Add tomatoes: Add chopped tomatoes to the pan along with turmeric powder, red chili powder, and salt. Mix well.
5. Cooking the chutney: Cook the tomatoes on medium heat, stirring occasionally, until they soften and break down. This will take about 10-15 minutes.
6. Simmer and adjust consistency: Once tomatoes are soft, add sugar or jaggery to balance the acidity. Stir well and simmer for another 5-10 minutes until the chutney thickens to your desired consistency.
7. Finish with tanginess (optional): If desired, add vinegar or lemon juice for a tangy kick. Adjust salt and sugar according to your taste preferences.
8. Cool and store: Let the chutney cool completely before transferring it to a clean, dry jar or container. It can be stored in the refrigerator for up to a week.

Serving suggestions:

- Serve tomato chutney with dosa, idli, uttapam, or other South Indian breakfast dishes.
- Use it as a spread for sandwiches or wraps.

- Enjoy it as a condiment with snacks like samosas, pakoras, or crackers.

This homemade tomato chutney is bursting with flavors from spices and tomatoes, making it a versatile and delicious addition to your meals. Adjust the spice levels and sweetness to suit your taste preferences.

Tomato and Avocado Salsa

Ingredients:

- 2 medium tomatoes, diced
- 1 avocado, diced
- 1/4 cup red onion, finely chopped
- 1 jalapeño or serrano chili, seeded and minced (optional, for heat)
- 1/4 cup fresh cilantro, chopped
- 1-2 tablespoons fresh lime juice (about 1 lime)
- Salt and pepper, to taste

Instructions:

1. Prepare the ingredients: Dice the tomatoes and avocado into small pieces. Finely chop the red onion, jalapeño or serrano chili (if using), and cilantro.
2. Combine ingredients: In a mixing bowl, gently toss together the diced tomatoes, diced avocado, chopped red onion, minced chili (if using), and chopped cilantro.
3. Add lime juice: Squeeze fresh lime juice over the mixture. Start with 1 tablespoon of lime juice and adjust to taste. The lime juice adds a tangy brightness and also helps to prevent the avocado from browning too quickly.
4. Season: Season the salsa with salt and pepper to taste. Mix gently to combine all the ingredients evenly.
5. Chill (optional): For best flavor, let the salsa sit in the refrigerator for about 15-30 minutes before serving to allow the flavors to meld together.
6. Serve: Transfer the tomato and avocado salsa to a serving bowl and serve immediately as a dip with tortilla chips, or use it as a topping for tacos, grilled chicken, fish, or any other dish you prefer.

Tips:

- Choose ripe but firm avocados for best results. If they are too ripe, they may turn mushy when mixed.
- Adjust the amount of chili according to your heat preference. You can also leave it out if you prefer a mild salsa.
- If you prefer a smoother texture, you can mash some of the avocado with a fork before mixing it with the other ingredients.

This tomato and avocado salsa is not only delicious but also healthy and full of fresh flavors. It's a versatile condiment that adds a burst of color and taste to your favorite dishes. Enjoy!

Tomato Pie

Ingredients:

- 1 prepared pie crust (store-bought or homemade)
- 4-5 medium-sized tomatoes, sliced (about 1/4-inch thick slices)
- 1 cup shredded mozzarella cheese
- 1/2 cup grated Parmesan cheese
- 1/2 cup mayonnaise
- 2-3 green onions, chopped
- 1/4 cup fresh basil, chopped (or 1 tablespoon dried basil)
- 1/4 cup fresh parsley, chopped (optional)
- Salt and pepper, to taste

Instructions:

1. Preheat your oven: Preheat oven to 375°F (190°C).
2. Prepare the pie crust: If using a store-bought pie crust, follow the package instructions for pre-baking (blind baking) or use a homemade pie crust. Bake the crust according to the instructions until lightly golden brown. Let it cool slightly.
3. Prepare the tomatoes: Slice the tomatoes about 1/4-inch thick. Place the slices on paper towels to drain excess liquid. Sprinkle lightly with salt and let sit for 10-15 minutes. Pat dry with paper towels to remove excess moisture.
4. Prepare the filling: In a medium bowl, combine the shredded mozzarella cheese, grated Parmesan cheese, mayonnaise, chopped green onions, chopped basil, chopped parsley (if using), salt, and pepper. Mix well until everything is evenly combined.
5. Assemble the pie: Spread a thin layer of the cheese mixture over the bottom of the baked pie crust. Layer the tomato slices on top, overlapping slightly if needed. Season the tomatoes with a bit of salt and pepper.
6. Add remaining filling: Spread the remaining cheese mixture evenly over the tomatoes, covering them completely.
7. Bake the pie: Place the assembled tomato pie on a baking sheet (to catch any drips) and bake in the preheated oven for 30-35 minutes, or until the filling is golden brown and bubbly.
8. Cool and serve: Remove the tomato pie from the oven and let it cool for about 10 minutes before slicing. Garnish with additional fresh basil or parsley if desired. Serve warm or at room temperature.

Tips:

- Use ripe tomatoes for the best flavor. You can use a variety of tomatoes for added color and taste.
- If you prefer a lighter version, you can use Greek yogurt instead of mayonnaise in the filling.

- Customize the herbs and seasonings to your taste. Thyme, oregano, or chives can also be great additions.

Tomato pie is a delightful dish that can be served as a main course or as a side dish alongside salads or grilled meats. It's perfect for summer when tomatoes are at their peak freshness. Enjoy your homemade tomato pie!

Tomato and Eggplant Parmesan

Ingredients:

- 2 medium-sized eggplants
- Salt
- 1 cup all-purpose flour
- 3 large eggs, beaten
- 2 cups breadcrumbs (or Italian-style breadcrumbs)
- 1/2 cup grated Parmesan cheese, plus extra for topping
- 2 cups marinara sauce (homemade or store-bought)
- 1 cup shredded mozzarella cheese
- Fresh basil leaves, chopped (for garnish, optional)
- Olive oil, for frying
- Freshly ground black pepper

Instructions:

1. Prepare the eggplant:
    - Trim off the ends of the eggplants and peel if desired (peeling is optional).
    - Slice the eggplants crosswise into 1/2-inch thick rounds.
    - Lay the slices on a baking sheet or large plate and sprinkle both sides generously with salt. Let them sit for about 30 minutes to draw out excess moisture.
2. Bread the eggplant slices:
    - Preheat the oven to 375°F (190°C).
    - Set up a breading station: Place the flour in one shallow dish, the beaten eggs in another dish, and combine the breadcrumbs with the grated Parmesan cheese in a third dish.
    - Pat the eggplant slices dry with paper towels to remove excess moisture.
    - Dredge each slice in the flour, shaking off any excess.
    - Dip the floured slices into the beaten eggs, allowing any excess to drip off.
    - Coat the slices evenly with the breadcrumb mixture, pressing gently to adhere.
3. Fry the eggplant slices:
    - In a large skillet, heat about 1/4 inch of olive oil over medium heat.
    - Working in batches, fry the breaded eggplant slices until golden brown and crispy on both sides, about 2-3 minutes per side.
    - Transfer the fried eggplant slices to a plate lined with paper towels to drain excess oil.
4. Assemble the Tomato and Eggplant Parmesan:
    - Spread a thin layer of marinara sauce on the bottom of a 9x13 inch baking dish.
    - Arrange a single layer of fried eggplant slices over the sauce.
    - Spoon more marinara sauce over the eggplant slices, spreading it evenly.
    - Sprinkle a layer of shredded mozzarella cheese over the sauce.

- Repeat the layers: eggplant slices, sauce, and mozzarella cheese, until all ingredients are used, ending with a layer of sauce and mozzarella cheese on top.

5. **Bake:**
    - Cover the baking dish loosely with aluminum foil to prevent the cheese from burning.
    - Bake in the preheated oven for 25-30 minutes.
    - Remove the foil and continue baking for another 10-15 minutes, or until the cheese is melted and bubbly.

6. **Serve:**
    - Let the Tomato and Eggplant Parmesan cool for a few minutes before slicing.
    - Garnish with freshly chopped basil and extra grated Parmesan cheese if desired.
    - Serve warm as a main dish with a side salad and crusty bread.

Tips:

- You can prepare the eggplant slices ahead of time and store them in the refrigerator until ready to assemble and bake.
- If you prefer a lighter version, you can bake the breaded eggplant slices instead of frying them. Arrange them on a baking sheet lined with parchment paper, drizzle with olive oil, and bake at 400°F (200°C) for about 20-25 minutes, flipping halfway through.
- Feel free to add other ingredients such as sliced fresh tomatoes or a sprinkle of dried oregano between the layers for extra flavor.

Enjoy this hearty and comforting Tomato and Eggplant Parmesan dish with its crispy, cheesy layers and rich tomato sauce!

Sun-Dried Tomato Pesto

Ingredients:

- 1 cup sun-dried tomatoes (dry-packed, not in oil)
- 1/2 cup fresh basil leaves
- 2 cloves garlic, peeled
- 1/3 cup grated Parmesan cheese
- 1/4 cup pine nuts or walnuts (toasted, if desired)
- 1/2 cup extra virgin olive oil
- Salt and pepper, to taste

Instructions:

1. Prepare the sun-dried tomatoes: If using sun-dried tomatoes that are dry-packed (not in oil), rehydrate them first by soaking in hot water for about 10-15 minutes until softened. Drain well.
2. Toast the nuts (if desired): In a dry skillet over medium heat, toast the pine nuts or walnuts until lightly golden and fragrant. Stir frequently to prevent burning. Remove from heat and let them cool slightly.
3. Combine ingredients: In a food processor, combine the sun-dried tomatoes (drained), fresh basil leaves, peeled garlic cloves, grated Parmesan cheese, and toasted nuts. Pulse several times until the ingredients are roughly chopped and blended.
4. Add olive oil: With the food processor running, slowly drizzle in the olive oil until the mixture becomes smooth and well combined. You may need to scrape down the sides of the processor bowl occasionally.
5. Season: Taste and season the sun-dried tomato pesto with salt and pepper to your liking. Adjust the consistency with more olive oil if you prefer a thinner pesto.
6. Store or serve: Transfer the sun-dried tomato pesto to a jar or container with a tight-fitting lid. Store in the refrigerator for up to one week. For longer storage, you can freeze the pesto in ice cube trays and then transfer the frozen cubes to a freezer bag.

Serving suggestions:

- Toss the sun-dried tomato pesto with cooked pasta, adding some reserved pasta water to loosen the sauce.
- Use it as a spread on sandwiches or wraps.
- Serve it as a dip for crusty bread or as a topping for bruschetta.
- Use it as a sauce for grilled chicken, fish, or vegetables.

Sun-dried tomato pesto adds a burst of robust flavor to any dish and is a great way to enjoy the intense sweetness of sun-dried tomatoes in a different form. Adjust the ingredients and seasonings to suit your taste preferences, and enjoy this delicious homemade pesto!

Tomato and Cucumber Salad

Ingredients:

- 2 large tomatoes, diced
- 1 cucumber, diced (English cucumber works well)
- 1/4 red onion, thinly sliced (optional)
- 1/4 cup fresh parsley or cilantro, chopped
- 2 tablespoons extra virgin olive oil
- 1 tablespoon red wine vinegar or lemon juice
- Salt and pepper, to taste

Optional additions:

- 1/2 cup crumbled feta cheese
- 1/4 cup sliced black olives
- 1/2 teaspoon dried oregano or basil
- 1/4 teaspoon crushed red pepper flakes (for a bit of heat)

Instructions:

1. Prepare the vegetables: Dice the tomatoes and cucumber into bite-sized pieces. If using red onion, thinly slice it. Chop the fresh parsley or cilantro.
2. Make the dressing: In a small bowl, whisk together the extra virgin olive oil and red wine vinegar (or lemon juice). Season with salt and pepper to taste.
3. Combine ingredients: In a large mixing bowl, combine the diced tomatoes, diced cucumber, sliced red onion (if using), and chopped parsley or cilantro.
4. Dress the salad: Pour the dressing over the vegetables and gently toss to coat evenly.
5. Chill (optional): For best flavor, let the salad chill in the refrigerator for about 15-30 minutes before serving to allow the flavors to meld together.
6. Serve: Transfer the tomato and cucumber salad to a serving bowl or platter. If desired, sprinkle with crumbled feta cheese, sliced black olives, dried herbs, or crushed red pepper flakes for added flavor and garnish.

Tips:

- Choose ripe and firm tomatoes for the best texture and flavor.
- English cucumbers are great for salads because they have thin skins and fewer seeds.
- Customize the salad by adding other vegetables like bell peppers or avocado.
- This salad is perfect as a side dish for grilled meats or fish, or as a light and refreshing lunch option on its own.

Enjoy this tomato and cucumber salad as a vibrant and healthy addition to your meals, especially during the summer months when tomatoes and cucumbers are at their peak freshness!

Tomato and Spinach Quiche

Ingredients:

- 1 pie crust (store-bought or homemade), unbaked
- 1 cup fresh spinach, chopped
- 1 cup cherry tomatoes, halved
- 1/2 cup shredded mozzarella cheese
- 1/2 cup shredded cheddar cheese (or any cheese of your choice)
- 4 large eggs
- 1 cup milk (whole milk or half-and-half)
- 1/2 teaspoon salt
- 1/4 teaspoon black pepper
- 1/4 teaspoon garlic powder
- 1/4 teaspoon dried thyme (optional)
- Olive oil, for sautéing spinach

Instructions:

1. Preheat your oven: Preheat oven to 375°F (190°C).
2. Prepare the pie crust: If using a store-bought pie crust, follow the package instructions for pre-baking (blind baking). If using a homemade pie crust, roll it out and fit it into a 9-inch pie dish. Crimp the edges and refrigerate while preparing the filling.
3. Prepare the spinach: In a skillet, heat a drizzle of olive oil over medium heat. Add the chopped spinach and sauté until wilted, about 2-3 minutes. Remove from heat and set aside.
4. Assemble the quiche:
    - Spread the sautéed spinach evenly over the bottom of the pie crust.
    - Scatter the halved cherry tomatoes over the spinach.
    - Sprinkle both cheeses (mozzarella and cheddar) over the spinach and tomatoes.
5. Prepare the egg mixture: In a mixing bowl, whisk together the eggs, milk, salt, pepper, garlic powder, and dried thyme (if using) until well combined.
6. Pour over the filling: Carefully pour the egg mixture over the spinach, tomatoes, and cheese in the pie crust.
7. Bake the quiche: Place the quiche on a baking sheet (to catch any spills) and bake in the preheated oven for 35-40 minutes, or until the quiche is set and the top is golden brown.
8. Cool and serve: Remove the quiche from the oven and let it cool for a few minutes before slicing. Serve warm or at room temperature.

Tips:

- You can customize this quiche by adding other ingredients such as cooked bacon, diced ham, sautéed mushrooms, or caramelized onions.
- For a vegetarian option, omit the meat and add more vegetables or greens.

- Make sure to let the quiche cool slightly before slicing to allow it to set properly.
- Leftovers can be stored in the refrigerator for up to 3 days. Reheat in the oven or microwave before serving.

This tomato and spinach quiche makes for a delicious brunch or light dinner option. It's versatile, satisfying, and perfect for using up fresh spinach and tomatoes from your garden or local market. Enjoy!

Tomato and Mozzarella Stuffed Chicken

Ingredients:

- 4 boneless, skinless chicken breasts
- Salt and pepper, to taste
- 4 slices mozzarella cheese
- 1 large tomato, sliced
- 1/4 cup fresh basil leaves, chopped
- 2 tablespoons olive oil
- 2 cloves garlic, minced
- 1/2 cup chicken broth or white wine
- 1/4 cup heavy cream (optional)
- Fresh basil leaves, for garnish

Instructions:

1. Prepare the chicken breasts:
   - Preheat your oven to 375°F (190°C).
   - Butterfly each chicken breast: Lay them flat on a cutting board and slice horizontally along the side to create a pocket without cutting all the way through. Season the inside and outside of the chicken breasts with salt and pepper.
2. Stuff the chicken breasts:
   - Place a slice of mozzarella cheese, a few slices of tomato, and a sprinkle of chopped basil inside each chicken breast pocket. Secure the openings with toothpicks if necessary.
3. Sear the chicken:
   - In a large oven-safe skillet, heat olive oil over medium-high heat. Add minced garlic and sauté for about 30 seconds until fragrant.
   - Add the stuffed chicken breasts to the skillet and sear on each side until golden brown, about 3-4 minutes per side.
4. Bake the chicken:
   - Transfer the skillet to the preheated oven and bake for 15-20 minutes, or until the chicken is cooked through (internal temperature of 165°F or 74°C).
5. Make the sauce (optional):
   - Remove the chicken breasts from the skillet and set aside on a plate, tented with foil to keep warm.
   - Deglaze the skillet with chicken broth or white wine, scraping up any browned bits from the bottom of the pan.
   - If using, stir in heavy cream and simmer until the sauce thickens slightly. Season with salt and pepper to taste.
6. Serve:
   - Spoon the sauce over the stuffed chicken breasts. Garnish with fresh basil leaves before serving.

Tips:

- Make sure to properly secure the chicken breast pockets with toothpicks to prevent the filling from spilling out during cooking.
- You can add additional herbs or seasonings to the filling according to your taste, such as dried Italian herbs or a sprinkle of red pepper flakes for heat.
- Serve the Tomato and Mozzarella Stuffed Chicken with a side of pasta, rice, or a crisp green salad for a complete meal.

This dish is perfect for a special dinner or when you want to impress with a flavorful and comforting chicken recipe. Enjoy the melty cheese and fresh tomato flavors stuffed inside tender chicken breasts!

Tomato and Corn Salad

Ingredients:

- 2 cups cherry tomatoes, halved (or diced tomatoes)
- 2 cups fresh corn kernels (about 2-3 ears of corn)
- 1/4 cup red onion, finely chopped (optional)
- 1/4 cup fresh basil, chopped
- 2 tablespoons extra virgin olive oil
- 1 tablespoon red wine vinegar or balsamic vinegar
- Salt and pepper, to taste

Optional additions:

- 1/4 cup crumbled feta cheese
- 1 avocado, diced
- 1/2 cup cucumber, diced
- 1 jalapeño pepper, seeded and minced (for a spicy kick)

Instructions:

1. Prepare the corn: If using fresh corn on the cob, shuck the corn and remove the silk. Bring a large pot of water to a boil and add the corn. Cook for about 3-5 minutes until the corn is tender. Remove from water and let cool. Once cooled, cut the kernels off the cob.
2. Prepare the salad: In a large bowl, combine the halved cherry tomatoes, fresh corn kernels, finely chopped red onion (if using), and chopped fresh basil.
3. Make the dressing: In a small bowl, whisk together the extra virgin olive oil and red wine vinegar or balsamic vinegar. Season with salt and pepper to taste.
4. Combine and toss: Pour the dressing over the tomato and corn mixture. Gently toss until everything is evenly coated with the dressing.
5. Optional additions: If desired, add crumbled feta cheese, diced avocado, diced cucumber, or minced jalapeño pepper to the salad. Toss gently to combine.
6. Chill (optional): For best flavor, let the salad chill in the refrigerator for about 15-30 minutes before serving to allow the flavors to meld together.
7. Serve: Transfer the Tomato and Corn Salad to a serving bowl or platter. Garnish with additional fresh basil leaves if desired.

Tips:

- Use ripe and juicy tomatoes for the best flavor. You can use a variety of tomatoes such as cherry tomatoes, grape tomatoes, or heirloom tomatoes.
- Customize the salad by adding other ingredients like black beans, bell peppers, or grilled corn for added texture and flavor.

- Adjust the amount of vinegar and olive oil based on your taste preferences. You can also add a pinch of sugar if you prefer a slightly sweeter dressing.
- This salad is perfect for picnics, barbecues, or as a side dish to grilled meats or seafood.

Enjoy this Tomato and Corn Salad as a vibrant and delicious addition to your summer meals!

Tomato and Lentil Soup

Ingredients:

- 1 cup dried lentils (brown or green lentils), rinsed and drained
- 1 tablespoon olive oil
- 1 onion, chopped
- 2 carrots, diced
- 2 celery stalks, diced
- 3 cloves garlic, minced
- 1 teaspoon dried thyme (or 1 tablespoon fresh thyme leaves)
- 1 teaspoon dried oregano
- 1/2 teaspoon smoked paprika (optional, for added flavor)
- 1/4 teaspoon red pepper flakes (optional, for heat)
- 1 can (28 ounces) diced tomatoes (or 4-5 fresh tomatoes, diced)
- 4 cups vegetable broth (or chicken broth)
- Salt and pepper, to taste
- Fresh parsley or basil, chopped (for garnish)

Instructions:

1. Prepare the lentils: Rinse the lentils under cold water and drain them. Set aside.
2. Sauté vegetables: In a large pot or Dutch oven, heat olive oil over medium heat. Add chopped onion, diced carrots, and diced celery. Sauté for about 5-7 minutes, or until the vegetables begin to soften.
3. Add garlic and spices: Add minced garlic, dried thyme, dried oregano, smoked paprika (if using), and red pepper flakes (if using). Cook for 1 minute until fragrant, stirring constantly.
4. Add tomatoes and lentils: Stir in the diced tomatoes (with their juices) and drained lentils. Mix well to combine with the vegetables and spices.
5. Simmer the soup: Pour in the vegetable broth (or chicken broth) and bring the mixture to a boil. Reduce the heat to low, cover partially with a lid, and let the soup simmer for about 25-30 minutes, or until the lentils are tender.
6. Season and adjust: Taste the soup and season with salt and pepper as needed, adjusting to your preference.
7. Serve: Ladle the Tomato and Lentil Soup into bowls. Garnish with chopped fresh parsley or basil before serving.

Tips:

- For a creamier texture, you can blend a portion of the soup using an immersion blender or transfer a portion to a blender, blend until smooth, and then return it to the pot.
- Add more broth if you prefer a thinner soup consistency.

- Customize the soup by adding additional vegetables such as spinach, kale, or bell peppers.
- This soup can be stored in the refrigerator for up to 4-5 days, making it a great option for meal prep.

Enjoy this hearty and nutritious Tomato and Lentil Soup as a comforting meal on its own or with crusty bread for dipping!

Tomato and Onion Gratin

Ingredients:

- 4 large tomatoes, sliced into 1/4-inch thick rounds
- 2 large onions, thinly sliced
- 2 tablespoons olive oil
- Salt and pepper, to taste
- 1 cup breadcrumbs (preferably fresh)
- 1/2 cup grated Parmesan cheese
- 1/4 cup chopped fresh parsley (optional)
- 2 cloves garlic, minced
- 2 tablespoons unsalted butter, melted

Instructions:

1. Preheat your oven: Preheat oven to 375°F (190°C).
2. Caramelize the onions: In a large skillet, heat olive oil over medium-low heat. Add the thinly sliced onions and cook, stirring occasionally, until they are caramelized and golden brown, about 20-25 minutes. Season with salt and pepper to taste. Remove from heat and set aside.
3. Prepare the tomatoes: Slice the tomatoes into 1/4-inch thick rounds. Season them lightly with salt and pepper.
4. Assemble the gratin:
    - In a small bowl, mix together the breadcrumbs, grated Parmesan cheese, chopped parsley (if using), minced garlic, and melted butter. Season with a pinch of salt and pepper.
    - In a baking dish (about 9x13 inches), arrange a layer of half of the caramelized onions.
    - Top the onions with half of the sliced tomatoes, slightly overlapping them.
    - Sprinkle half of the breadcrumb mixture over the tomatoes.
    - Repeat with another layer of the remaining caramelized onions, sliced tomatoes, and finish with the remaining breadcrumb mixture on top.
5. Bake the gratin: Cover the baking dish loosely with aluminum foil and bake in the preheated oven for 20 minutes. Then, remove the foil and bake for an additional 10-15 minutes, or until the top is golden brown and the tomatoes are tender.
6. Serve: Remove the Tomato and Onion Gratin from the oven and let it cool slightly before serving. Garnish with additional chopped parsley if desired.

Tips:

- Choose ripe and firm tomatoes for the best texture and flavor in the gratin.
- You can use any type of breadcrumbs, but fresh breadcrumbs will give a crispier and more flavorful topping.

- If you prefer a stronger cheese flavor, you can substitute or mix in other cheeses like Gruyère or mozzarella.
- Serve the Tomato and Onion Gratin as a side dish alongside grilled meats or fish, or enjoy it as a vegetarian main dish with a side salad.

This Tomato and Onion Gratin is a comforting and flavorful dish that highlights the sweetness of tomatoes and the richness of caramelized onions. It's perfect for both casual dinners and special occasions. Enjoy!

Tomato and Feta Couscous

Ingredients:

- 1 cup couscous
- 1 1/4 cups vegetable or chicken broth (or water)
- 1 tablespoon olive oil
- 1 pint cherry tomatoes, halved
- 1/2 cup crumbled feta cheese
- 1/4 cup fresh basil leaves, chopped
- 1/4 cup fresh parsley leaves, chopped
- 2 tablespoons lemon juice
- Salt and pepper, to taste

Instructions:

1. Cook the couscous:
    - In a medium saucepan, bring the vegetable or chicken broth (or water) to a boil.
    - Stir in the couscous and olive oil. Remove from heat, cover, and let it sit for 5 minutes, allowing the couscous to absorb the liquid.
2. Fluff the couscous: After 5 minutes, uncover the saucepan and fluff the couscous with a fork to separate the grains.
3. Prepare the tomatoes and herbs:
    - In a large bowl, combine the halved cherry tomatoes, crumbled feta cheese, chopped fresh basil, and chopped fresh parsley.
4. Combine the ingredients:
    - Add the cooked couscous to the bowl with the tomatoes, feta, and herbs.
    - Drizzle with lemon juice and gently toss to combine all the ingredients evenly.
5. Season:
    - Season the Tomato and Feta Couscous with salt and pepper to taste. Adjust lemon juice or olive oil if desired.
6. Serve:
    - Serve the Tomato and Feta Couscous warm or at room temperature as a side dish or a light main dish.
    - Garnish with additional fresh herbs if desired.

Tips:

- You can customize this dish by adding other ingredients such as diced cucumber, olives, or red onion for extra crunch and flavor.
- For a Mediterranean twist, sprinkle some dried oregano or crumble some dried mint over the couscous.
- Use Israeli couscous (pearl couscous) instead of regular couscous for a different texture.

This Tomato and Feta Couscous is quick to prepare and bursting with fresh flavors. It makes a great side dish for grilled meats or fish, or as a standalone vegetarian option. Enjoy this dish for its simplicity and delicious combination of ingredients!

Tomato and Pancetta Risotto

Ingredients:

- 1 cup Arborio rice
- 4 cups chicken or vegetable broth, kept warm
- 1/2 cup dry white wine
- 1/2 cup diced pancetta (or bacon)
- 1 small onion, finely chopped
- 2 cloves garlic, minced
- 1 cup cherry tomatoes, halved
- 1/2 cup grated Parmesan cheese, plus extra for serving
- 2 tablespoons tomato paste
- 2 tablespoons unsalted butter
- 2 tablespoons olive oil
- Salt and pepper, to taste
- Fresh basil or parsley, chopped (for garnish)

Instructions:

1. Prepare the broth: In a saucepan, heat the chicken or vegetable broth over low heat to keep it warm while you prepare the risotto.
2. Cook the pancetta: In a large skillet or Dutch oven, heat 1 tablespoon of olive oil over medium heat. Add the diced pancetta and cook until crispy, about 5-7 minutes. Remove the pancetta from the skillet and drain on paper towels. Set aside.
3. Sauté onion and garlic: In the same skillet, add the remaining tablespoon of olive oil. Add the finely chopped onion and sauté for 3-4 minutes until translucent. Add the minced garlic and cook for another 1 minute until fragrant.
4. Toast the rice: Add the Arborio rice to the skillet with the onion and garlic. Stir to coat the rice with the oil and toast for 1-2 minutes until the rice becomes translucent around the edges.
5. Deglaze with wine: Pour in the white wine and stir constantly until it is absorbed by the rice.
6. Add tomatoes and tomato paste: Stir in the halved cherry tomatoes and tomato paste. Cook for 1-2 minutes, allowing the tomatoes to soften slightly.
7. Cook the risotto: Begin adding the warm broth to the skillet, one ladleful (about 1/2 cup) at a time, stirring frequently. Allow each addition of broth to be absorbed by the rice before adding the next ladleful. Continue this process for about 18-20 minutes, or until the rice is creamy and al dente.
8. Finish the risotto: Stir in the grated Parmesan cheese, cooked pancetta, and unsalted butter until melted and well combined. Season with salt and pepper to taste.
9. Serve: Divide the Tomato and Pancetta Risotto among serving plates. Garnish with additional grated Parmesan cheese and chopped fresh basil or parsley.

Tips:

- Stirring frequently while adding broth helps release the starch from the rice, creating a creamy texture in the risotto.
- Use good quality Arborio rice for the best results. It absorbs liquid well and creates a creamy consistency.
- If you prefer a smoother tomato flavor, you can use tomato passata or crushed tomatoes instead of cherry tomatoes and tomato paste.
- Serve the risotto immediately as it continues to absorb liquid and can become dry upon standing.

Enjoy this Tomato and Pancetta Risotto as a comforting and flavorful main dish or side dish, perfect for a special dinner or any day of the week!

Tomato and Basil Bruschetta

Ingredients:

- 4-5 ripe tomatoes, diced
- 1/4 cup fresh basil leaves, thinly sliced (chiffonade)
- 2 cloves garlic, minced
- 1 tablespoon balsamic vinegar
- 2 tablespoons extra virgin olive oil, plus extra for drizzling
- Salt and pepper, to taste
- 1 baguette or Italian bread, sliced into 1/2-inch thick slices
- Optional: 1-2 cloves of garlic, peeled (for rubbing on the bread)

Instructions:

1. Prepare the tomatoes: In a medium bowl, combine the diced tomatoes, thinly sliced basil leaves, minced garlic, balsamic vinegar, and extra virgin olive oil. Season with salt and pepper to taste. Mix well and set aside to marinate for at least 15-20 minutes to allow the flavors to meld together.
2. Toast the bread slices: Preheat the oven to 375°F (190°C). Place the bread slices on a baking sheet in a single layer. Drizzle or brush both sides of each slice with olive oil. Optionally, rub one side of each slice with a peeled garlic clove for extra flavor.
3. Bake the bread: Bake the bread slices in the preheated oven for about 8-10 minutes, or until they are golden and crispy. Remove from the oven and let them cool slightly.
4. Assemble the bruschetta: Spoon the tomato and basil mixture generously over each toasted bread slice. Make sure to include some of the juices from the tomato mixture.
5. Serve: Arrange the Tomato and Basil Bruschetta on a serving platter and serve immediately.

Tips:

- Choose ripe and flavorful tomatoes for the best bruschetta. Roma tomatoes or cherry tomatoes work well.
- If you prefer a more pronounced garlic flavor, you can mix minced garlic directly into the tomato mixture or rub the toasted bread slices with a peeled garlic clove before adding the tomato mixture.
- You can customize your bruschetta by adding toppings like fresh mozzarella slices, prosciutto, or a drizzle of balsamic glaze.

This Tomato and Basil Bruschetta is perfect for serving as an appetizer at parties, gatherings, or as a light and flavorful snack. Enjoy the vibrant flavors of tomatoes and basil on crunchy toasted bread!

Tomato and Garlic Shrimp

Ingredients:

- 1 pound large shrimp, peeled and deveined
- 2 tablespoons olive oil
- 4 cloves garlic, minced
- 1 pint cherry tomatoes, halved
- 1/2 cup chicken broth or white wine
- 1/4 teaspoon red pepper flakes (optional, for heat)
- Salt and pepper, to taste
- 2 tablespoons fresh parsley, chopped
- Cooked pasta or crusty bread, for serving

Instructions:

1. Prepare the shrimp: Pat the shrimp dry with paper towels and season with salt and pepper.
2. Cook the shrimp: In a large skillet, heat olive oil over medium-high heat. Add the shrimp in a single layer and cook for about 2 minutes per side, until pink and opaque. Remove the shrimp from the skillet and set aside.
3. Sauté garlic and tomatoes: In the same skillet, add minced garlic and sauté for about 30 seconds until fragrant. Add the halved cherry tomatoes and cook for 2-3 minutes, stirring occasionally, until they begin to soften.
4. Deglaze the skillet: Pour in the chicken broth or white wine, scraping up any browned bits from the bottom of the skillet. Add red pepper flakes if using. Bring to a simmer and cook for another 2-3 minutes until the sauce slightly thickens.
5. Combine shrimp with sauce: Return the cooked shrimp to the skillet. Toss gently with the tomato and garlic mixture until the shrimp are coated and heated through.
6. Finish and serve: Remove the skillet from heat. Sprinkle with chopped fresh parsley and season with additional salt and pepper if needed. Serve the Tomato and Garlic Shrimp immediately over cooked pasta or with crusty bread for soaking up the delicious sauce.

Tips:

- Use fresh, ripe cherry tomatoes for the best flavor and texture in the dish.
- Adjust the amount of red pepper flakes according to your preference for spiciness.
- Feel free to add extra vegetables such as spinach or bell peppers for additional flavor and color.
- For a creamy variation, you can add a splash of heavy cream or a dollop of cream cheese to the sauce before adding the shrimp back to the skillet.

This Tomato and Garlic Shrimp dish is quick and easy to prepare, making it perfect for weeknight dinners or special occasions. Enjoy the savory combination of shrimp, tomatoes, and garlic in every bite!

Tomato and Herb Focaccia

Ingredients:

For the dough:

- 4 cups all-purpose flour
- 2 teaspoons salt
- 1 tablespoon granulated sugar
- 1 tablespoon instant yeast
- 1 1/2 cups warm water (about 110°F or 45°C)
- 1/4 cup olive oil, plus extra for drizzling

For topping:

- 1-2 tomatoes, thinly sliced
- Fresh herbs (rosemary, thyme, oregano), chopped
- Coarse sea salt, for sprinkling
- Black pepper, to taste
- Optional: garlic cloves, thinly sliced

Instructions:

1. Prepare the dough:
    - In a large mixing bowl, combine the flour, salt, sugar, and instant yeast. Mix well.
    - Make a well in the center of the dry ingredients and pour in the warm water and olive oil. Stir with a wooden spoon until a shaggy dough forms.
2. Knead the dough:
    - Transfer the dough to a floured surface and knead for about 8-10 minutes until the dough is smooth and elastic. Alternatively, you can knead the dough using a stand mixer with a dough hook attachment for 5-7 minutes.
3. First rise:
    - Place the dough in a lightly oiled bowl, turning to coat all sides with oil. Cover the bowl with a clean kitchen towel or plastic wrap.
    - Let the dough rise in a warm, draft-free place for 1-1.5 hours, or until doubled in size.
4. Prepare the focaccia:
    - Preheat your oven to 425°F (220°C). Grease a baking sheet or line it with parchment paper.
    - Punch down the risen dough and transfer it to the prepared baking sheet. Gently press and stretch the dough to fit the pan, creating dimples with your fingertips.
    - Drizzle olive oil generously over the top of the dough. Use your fingertips to spread the oil evenly over the surface.
5. Top the focaccia:

- Arrange the thinly sliced tomatoes evenly over the dough. Scatter the chopped fresh herbs and optional sliced garlic cloves over the tomatoes.
- Season with coarse sea salt and black pepper to taste. Drizzle a little more olive oil over the top.

6. Second rise:
   - Cover the focaccia loosely with a clean kitchen towel and let it rise again for about 20-30 minutes.
7. Bake the focaccia:
   - Place the focaccia in the preheated oven and bake for 20-25 minutes, or until the top is golden brown and the bread sounds hollow when tapped on the bottom.
   - Remove from the oven and transfer the focaccia to a wire rack to cool slightly before slicing.
8. Serve:
   - Slice the Tomato and Herb Focaccia and serve warm or at room temperature. Enjoy the bread on its own or as a side to soups, salads, or as an appetizer.

Tips:

- You can customize the herbs based on your preference. Besides rosemary, thyme, and oregano, basil or sage also work well.
- If you prefer a stronger garlic flavor, you can mix thinly sliced garlic cloves with the herbs and tomatoes before topping the focaccia.
- Store any leftovers in an airtight container at room temperature for up to 2 days. To reheat, wrap in aluminum foil and warm in the oven.

This Tomato and Herb Focaccia is perfect for sharing with friends and family. It's a wonderful combination of crispy exterior, soft interior, and bursting with flavors from the tomatoes and herbs. Enjoy baking this delicious bread!

Tomato and Zucchini Tian

Ingredients:

- 2-3 medium zucchini, thinly sliced
- 4-5 ripe tomatoes, thinly sliced
- 2 cloves garlic, minced
- 1/4 cup grated Parmesan cheese
- 1/4 cup breadcrumbs
- 2 tablespoons olive oil
- 1 tablespoon fresh thyme leaves (or 1 teaspoon dried thyme)
- 1 tablespoon fresh basil, chopped
- Salt and pepper, to taste

Instructions:

1. Preheat the oven: Preheat your oven to 375°F (190°C). Lightly grease a baking dish with olive oil or cooking spray.
2. Prepare the vegetables: Thinly slice the zucchini and tomatoes into rounds, about 1/4-inch thick. You can use a mandoline slicer for even slices.
3. Layer the vegetables: Arrange the zucchini and tomato slices in alternating layers in the prepared baking dish, overlapping slightly. You can layer them in a spiral pattern or any pattern you prefer.
4. Season the tian: Sprinkle minced garlic evenly over the layered vegetables. Drizzle olive oil over the top. Season with salt, pepper, fresh thyme leaves (or dried thyme), and chopped fresh basil.
5. Top with cheese and breadcrumbs: In a small bowl, mix together the grated Parmesan cheese and breadcrumbs. Sprinkle the mixture evenly over the top of the vegetables.
6. Bake the tian: Cover the baking dish with foil and bake in the preheated oven for 30 minutes. Then, remove the foil and bake for an additional 15-20 minutes, or until the vegetables are tender and the top is golden brown.
7. Serve: Remove the Tomato and Zucchini Tian from the oven and let it cool slightly before serving. Garnish with additional fresh herbs if desired.

Tips:

- Choose ripe but firm tomatoes and medium-sized zucchini for best results in texture and flavor.
- Feel free to add other herbs or spices such as rosemary, oregano, or red pepper flakes for added flavor.
- Serve the Tomato and Zucchini Tian as a side dish to grilled meats or fish, or as a vegetarian main dish with a side of crusty bread or salad.

This Tomato and Zucchini Tian is not only delicious but also a healthy and colorful addition to any meal. Enjoy the layers of flavors and textures in this simple yet elegant dish!

Tomato and Artichoke Pizza

Ingredients:

For the pizza dough:

- 1 pound pizza dough (store-bought or homemade)
- Cornmeal or flour, for dusting

For the toppings:

- 1/2 cup pizza sauce or marinara sauce
- 1 cup shredded mozzarella cheese
- 1/2 cup grated Parmesan cheese
- 1 cup marinated artichoke hearts, drained and quartered
- 1 cup cherry tomatoes, halved
- 2 tablespoons chopped fresh basil
- 1 tablespoon chopped fresh parsley
- Crushed red pepper flakes, to taste (optional)
- Salt and pepper, to taste
- Olive oil, for drizzling

Instructions:

1. Preheat the oven: Preheat your oven to the highest temperature setting (usually around 475°F to 500°F or as high as your oven will go). If using a pizza stone, place it in the oven while preheating.
2. Prepare the pizza dough: On a lightly floured surface, roll out the pizza dough to your desired thickness. Transfer the dough to a pizza peel or baking sheet dusted with cornmeal or flour.
3. Assemble the pizza:
    - Spread the pizza sauce evenly over the dough, leaving a small border around the edges for the crust.
    - Sprinkle the shredded mozzarella cheese and grated Parmesan cheese over the sauce.
    - Evenly distribute the quartered artichoke hearts and halved cherry tomatoes over the cheese.
    - Season with salt, pepper, and crushed red pepper flakes (if using). Sprinkle chopped fresh basil and parsley on top.
4. Bake the pizza:
    - If using a pizza stone, carefully slide the pizza onto the preheated stone in the oven. If using a baking sheet, place the baking sheet directly in the oven.
    - Bake the pizza for about 10-12 minutes, or until the crust is golden brown and the cheese is melted and bubbly.
5. Finish and serve:

- Remove the pizza from the oven and let it cool slightly. Drizzle with a little olive oil and sprinkle with additional fresh herbs if desired.
- Slice the Tomato and Artichoke Pizza and serve hot.

Tips:

- For a crispier crust, preheat your pizza stone in the oven before placing the pizza on it.
- Customize your pizza by adding other toppings such as sliced olives, red onion, or roasted garlic.
- If you prefer a vegetarian version, ensure the cheese you use is vegetarian-friendly (rennet-free).

This Tomato and Artichoke Pizza is perfect for pizza night at home or for entertaining guests. Enjoy the combination of flavors and textures in every bite of this delicious pizza!

Tomato and Pesto Crostini

Ingredients:

- 1 baguette, sliced into 1/2-inch thick rounds
- 1/4 cup olive oil
- 1 cup cherry tomatoes, halved
- 1/2 cup basil pesto (store-bought or homemade)
- Salt and pepper, to taste
- Optional: Balsamic glaze or reduction, for drizzling
- Fresh basil leaves, for garnish

Instructions:

1. Prepare the baguette slices:
   - Preheat your oven to 375°F (190°C). Arrange the baguette slices in a single layer on a baking sheet.
   - Brush both sides of each slice with olive oil. You can also drizzle olive oil over the slices if preferred.
2. Toast the baguette slices:
   - Bake in the preheated oven for 8-10 minutes, or until the bread is crispy and lightly golden brown. Remove from the oven and let them cool slightly.
3. Assemble the crostini:
   - Spread a thin layer of basil pesto onto each toasted baguette slice.
   - Top each crostini with halved cherry tomatoes. Arrange them evenly and press gently into the pesto.
4. Season and garnish:
   - Season the Tomato and Pesto Crostini with a pinch of salt and pepper to taste.
   - Optionally, drizzle a small amount of balsamic glaze or reduction over the crostini for added sweetness and flavor.
   - Garnish each crostini with fresh basil leaves for a pop of color and extra freshness.
5. Serve:
   - Arrange the Tomato and Pesto Crostini on a serving platter and serve immediately.

Tips:

- For extra flavor, you can rub the toasted baguette slices with a clove of garlic before brushing with olive oil.
- Customize the crostini by adding toppings such as mozzarella cheese, olives, or a sprinkle of grated Parmesan before baking.
- Make sure to use fresh and ripe cherry tomatoes for the best flavor in the crostini.

This Tomato and Pesto Crostini makes a fantastic appetizer for parties, gatherings, or as a starter before a meal. Enjoy the vibrant flavors of basil pesto and tomatoes on crispy toasted bread!

Tomato and Mushroom Risotto

Ingredients:

- 1 cup Arborio rice
- 4 cups vegetable or chicken broth (keep warm in a separate saucepan)
- 2 tablespoons olive oil
- 1 small onion, finely chopped
- 2 cloves garlic, minced
- 8 oz (225g) mushrooms (cremini or button), sliced
- 1 cup cherry tomatoes, halved
- 1/2 cup dry white wine
- 1/2 cup grated Parmesan cheese
- 2 tablespoons tomato paste
- 2 tablespoons unsalted butter
- Salt and pepper, to taste
- Fresh basil or parsley, chopped (for garnish)

Instructions:

1. Sauté the mushrooms: In a large skillet or Dutch oven, heat 1 tablespoon of olive oil over medium heat. Add the sliced mushrooms and cook until they are golden brown and all the moisture has evaporated, about 5-7 minutes. Remove the mushrooms from the skillet and set aside.
2. Prepare the risotto base: In the same skillet, add the remaining tablespoon of olive oil. Add the chopped onion and sauté for 3-4 minutes until translucent. Add the minced garlic and cook for another minute until fragrant.
3. Toast the rice: Add the Arborio rice to the skillet with the onions and garlic. Stir to coat the rice with the oil and toast for 1-2 minutes until the rice becomes translucent around the edges.
4. Deglaze with wine: Pour in the white wine and stir constantly until it is absorbed by the rice.
5. Cook the risotto: Begin adding the warm broth to the skillet, one ladleful (about 1/2 cup) at a time, stirring frequently. Allow each addition of broth to be absorbed by the rice before adding the next ladleful. Continue this process for about 18-20 minutes, or until the rice is creamy and al dente.
6. Add tomatoes and mushrooms: Stir in the halved cherry tomatoes, cooked mushrooms, and tomato paste. Cook for another 2-3 minutes, allowing the tomatoes to soften slightly and the flavors to meld.
7. Finish the risotto: Stir in the grated Parmesan cheese and unsalted butter until melted and well combined. Season with salt and pepper to taste.
8. Serve: Remove the Tomato and Mushroom Risotto from heat. Garnish with chopped fresh basil or parsley.

Tips:

- Use low-sodium broth to control the saltiness of the risotto.
- You can add a splash of heavy cream or a dollop of mascarpone cheese at the end for extra creaminess.
- Garnish with additional grated Parmesan cheese and a drizzle of good quality olive oil before serving.

This Tomato and Mushroom Risotto is creamy, flavorful, and perfect for a comforting meal. Enjoy the combination of tomatoes, mushrooms, and creamy rice in every bite!

Tomato and Sausage Pasta

Ingredients:

- 12 oz (340g) pasta of your choice (such as penne, fusilli, or spaghetti)
- 1 tablespoon olive oil
- 1 lb (450g) Italian sausage, casings removed
- 1 onion, finely chopped
- 3 cloves garlic, minced
- 1 can (14.5 oz / 400g) diced tomatoes
- 1 can (8 oz / 227g) tomato sauce
- 1 teaspoon dried oregano
- 1/2 teaspoon dried basil
- 1/4 teaspoon red pepper flakes (optional, for heat)
- Salt and pepper, to taste
- Fresh basil leaves, chopped, for garnish
- Grated Parmesan cheese, for serving

Instructions:

1. Cook the pasta: Cook the pasta in a large pot of salted boiling water according to package instructions until al dente. Drain and set aside, reserving about 1/2 cup of pasta water.
2. Prepare the sauce:
    - In a large skillet or Dutch oven, heat olive oil over medium heat. Add the Italian sausage, breaking it up with a spoon, and cook until browned and cooked through, about 5-7 minutes. Remove the sausage from the skillet and set aside.
3. Sauté onion and garlic: In the same skillet, add the finely chopped onion. Cook for 3-4 minutes until softened and translucent. Add the minced garlic and cook for another minute until fragrant.
4. Combine tomatoes and sauce: Stir in the diced tomatoes (with their juices) and tomato sauce into the skillet. Add dried oregano, dried basil, and red pepper flakes if using. Season with salt and pepper to taste.
5. Simmer the sauce: Bring the sauce to a simmer. Reduce the heat to low and let it simmer for 10-15 minutes, stirring occasionally, to allow the flavors to meld together and the sauce to thicken slightly.
6. Add sausage and pasta: Return the cooked Italian sausage to the skillet. Add the cooked pasta and toss everything together until well combined. If the sauce is too thick, add some of the reserved pasta water to loosen it up.
7. Serve: Remove from heat and garnish with chopped fresh basil leaves. Serve hot, topped with grated Parmesan cheese if desired.

Tips:

- Use sweet or spicy Italian sausage based on your preference.
- For a richer sauce, you can add a splash of heavy cream or a tablespoon of butter at the end.
- Customize the dish with additional vegetables such as bell peppers or spinach for added flavor and nutrition.

This Tomato and Sausage Pasta is a satisfying and comforting meal that the whole family will enjoy. Serve it with a side of garlic bread and a fresh green salad for a complete dinner!

Tomato and Olive Tapenade

Ingredients:

- 1 cup cherry tomatoes, halved
- 1/2 cup pitted black olives (Kalamata or similar), chopped
- 2 tablespoons capers, drained and chopped
- 2 cloves garlic, minced
- 1 tablespoon fresh lemon juice
- 2 tablespoons fresh basil, chopped
- 2 tablespoons fresh parsley, chopped
- 2 tablespoons olive oil
- Salt and pepper, to taste

Instructions:

1. Prepare the ingredients: Halve the cherry tomatoes, chop the pitted black olives and capers, mince the garlic, and chop the fresh basil and parsley.
2. Combine the ingredients: In a bowl, combine the cherry tomatoes, black olives, capers, minced garlic, fresh lemon juice, chopped basil, and chopped parsley.
3. Mix in olive oil: Drizzle olive oil over the mixture. Stir well to combine all ingredients evenly.
4. Season to taste: Season with salt and pepper to taste. Adjust lemon juice and olive oil as needed for desired flavor and consistency.
5. Chill and serve: Cover the bowl and refrigerate the Tomato and Olive Tapenade for at least 30 minutes to allow the flavors to meld together.
6. Serve: Serve the tapenade as a spread on crusty bread or crackers, or use it as a topping for grilled meats, fish, or vegetables. It can also be used as a flavorful addition to pasta or salads.

Tips:

- For a smoother consistency, pulse the ingredients in a food processor until desired texture is achieved.
- Add a pinch of crushed red pepper flakes for a hint of heat, if desired.
- Store leftover tapenade in an airtight container in the refrigerator for up to one week.

This Tomato and Olive Tapenade is versatile and adds a burst of Mediterranean flavors to various dishes. Enjoy its tangy, savory profile as a snack or as part of your favorite meal!

Tomato and Chickpea Stew

Ingredients:

- 2 tablespoons olive oil
- 1 onion, diced
- 3 cloves garlic, minced
- 1 red bell pepper, diced
- 1 teaspoon ground cumin
- 1 teaspoon ground coriander
- 1/2 teaspoon smoked paprika
- 1/4 teaspoon cayenne pepper (optional, for heat)
- 1 can (15 oz / 425g) chickpeas, drained and rinsed
- 1 can (14.5 oz / 411g) diced tomatoes
- 1 cup vegetable broth or water
- 1 tablespoon tomato paste
- Salt and pepper, to taste
- Fresh parsley or cilantro, chopped, for garnish
- Lemon wedges, for serving

Instructions:

1. Sauté aromatics: In a large pot or Dutch oven, heat olive oil over medium heat. Add the diced onion and cook for 3-4 minutes until softened.
2. Add spices: Stir in the minced garlic, diced red bell pepper, ground cumin, ground coriander, smoked paprika, and cayenne pepper (if using). Cook for 1-2 minutes until fragrant, stirring constantly.
3. Combine chickpeas and tomatoes: Add the drained and rinsed chickpeas, diced tomatoes (with their juices), vegetable broth or water, and tomato paste to the pot. Stir well to combine.
4. Simmer the stew: Bring the stew to a simmer. Reduce the heat to low, cover, and let it simmer for 15-20 minutes to allow the flavors to meld together and the stew to thicken slightly. Stir occasionally.
5. Season to taste: Taste and adjust seasoning with salt and pepper as needed.
6. Serve: Ladle the Tomato and Chickpea Stew into bowls. Garnish with chopped fresh parsley or cilantro. Serve with lemon wedges on the side for squeezing over the stew before eating.

Tips:

- For added richness, you can swirl in a tablespoon of butter or a splash of coconut milk at the end of cooking.
- Customize the stew by adding spinach or kale during the last few minutes of simmering for extra greens.

- This stew pairs well with crusty bread, rice, or couscous for a complete meal.

Enjoy this Tomato and Chickpea Stew as a comforting and nutritious dish, perfect for chilly days or anytime you crave a satisfying meal!

Tomato and Herb Quinoa

Ingredients:

- 1 cup quinoa, rinsed well
- 2 cups vegetable broth or water
- 1 tablespoon olive oil
- 1 onion, finely chopped
- 2 cloves garlic, minced
- 1 red bell pepper, diced
- 1 can (14.5 oz / 411g) diced tomatoes, drained
- 1/4 cup fresh basil, chopped
- 1/4 cup fresh parsley, chopped
- Salt and pepper, to taste
- Optional: Grated Parmesan cheese, for serving

Instructions:

1. Cook the quinoa: In a medium saucepan, bring the vegetable broth or water to a boil. Add the rinsed quinoa, reduce heat to low, cover, and simmer for 15-20 minutes, or until the quinoa is cooked and liquid is absorbed. Remove from heat and let it sit covered for 5 minutes. Fluff with a fork.
2. Sauté aromatics: While the quinoa is cooking, heat olive oil in a large skillet over medium heat. Add the chopped onion and cook for 3-4 minutes until softened.
3. Add vegetables: Stir in the minced garlic and diced red bell pepper. Cook for another 2-3 minutes until the bell pepper is tender.
4. Combine with tomatoes: Add the drained diced tomatoes to the skillet with the cooked vegetables. Stir well and cook for 2-3 minutes until heated through.
5. Mix in quinoa and herbs: Add the cooked quinoa to the skillet with the vegetables and tomatoes. Stir to combine thoroughly.
6. Season and garnish: Season the Tomato and Herb Quinoa with salt and pepper to taste. Stir in the chopped fresh basil and parsley.
7. Serve: Transfer the Tomato and Herb Quinoa to a serving dish. Serve warm, optionally topped with grated Parmesan cheese if desired.

Tips:

- For added protein, stir in cooked chickpeas, black beans, or grilled chicken strips.
- Customize the dish with other vegetables such as spinach, zucchini, or mushrooms.
- Drizzle with a little extra olive oil or a squeeze of lemon juice before serving for added freshness.

This Tomato and Herb Quinoa is a delicious and wholesome dish that can be served as a side or as a main course for a nutritious meal. Enjoy the flavors of fresh herbs and tomatoes combined with fluffy quinoa!

Tomato and Bacon Jam

Ingredients:

- 1 lb (450g) bacon, chopped into small pieces
- 1 onion, finely chopped
- 2 cloves garlic, minced
- 1/2 cup brown sugar
- 1/4 cup apple cider vinegar
- 1 can (14.5 oz / 411g) diced tomatoes, drained
- 1/4 teaspoon red pepper flakes (optional, for a hint of heat)
- Salt and black pepper, to taste

Instructions:

1. Cook the bacon: In a large skillet or Dutch oven, cook the chopped bacon over medium heat until it starts to brown and crisp, about 8-10 minutes.
2. Sauté onion and garlic: Add the finely chopped onion to the skillet with the bacon. Cook, stirring occasionally, for 5-6 minutes until the onion becomes translucent and starts to caramelize. Add the minced garlic and cook for another minute until fragrant.
3. Add sugar and vinegar: Sprinkle the brown sugar over the bacon mixture and stir to combine. Pour in the apple cider vinegar and stir well, scraping any browned bits from the bottom of the skillet.
4. Simmer with tomatoes: Stir in the drained diced tomatoes and red pepper flakes (if using). Bring the mixture to a simmer.
5. Cook until thickened: Reduce the heat to low and let the mixture simmer gently, stirring occasionally, for about 1 hour or until the jam has thickened to a spreadable consistency. Adjust the heat as needed to maintain a gentle simmer.
6. Season to taste: Taste the Tomato and Bacon Jam and season with salt and black pepper to taste. Adjust sweetness or acidity by adding more sugar or vinegar if desired.
7. Cool and store: Remove the skillet from heat and let the jam cool slightly. Transfer to clean, sterilized jars or airtight containers. Store in the refrigerator for up to 2 weeks.

Serving Suggestions:

- Spread Tomato and Bacon Jam on toasted bread or bagels for a delicious breakfast or snack.
- Use it as a condiment for sandwiches and burgers, especially with grilled meats or cheese.
- Serve it alongside cheese platters with crackers or crusty bread for a savory-sweet appetizer.

This Tomato and Bacon Jam recipe is versatile and adds a burst of flavor to various dishes. Enjoy its rich and savory profile with the sweetness from tomatoes and caramelized onions!

Tomato and Ricotta Gnocchi

Ingredients:

For the Gnocchi:

- 2 large russet potatoes (about 1 lb or 450g), scrubbed clean
- 1 cup whole milk ricotta cheese
- 1/2 cup grated Parmesan cheese
- 1 large egg
- 1 teaspoon salt
- 1/4 teaspoon black pepper
- Pinch of nutmeg (optional)
- 1 1/2 - 2 cups all-purpose flour, plus extra for dusting

For the Tomato Sauce:

- 2 tablespoons olive oil
- 3 cloves garlic, minced
- 1 can (14.5 oz / 411g) diced tomatoes
- 1/2 teaspoon dried oregano
- 1/2 teaspoon dried basil
- Salt and pepper, to taste
- Fresh basil leaves, chopped, for garnish
- Grated Parmesan cheese, for serving

Instructions:

To make the Gnocchi:

1. Cook the potatoes: Place the scrubbed potatoes in a large pot of salted water. Bring to a boil and cook until the potatoes are fork-tender, about 20-25 minutes. Drain well and let them cool slightly.
2. Prepare the dough: Peel the potatoes while they are still warm (use a kitchen towel to hold them if too hot). Mash the potatoes or pass them through a potato ricer onto a clean work surface or large bowl. Let them cool completely.
3. Form the dough: Add the ricotta cheese, grated Parmesan cheese, egg, salt, pepper, and nutmeg (if using) to the mashed potatoes. Mix well until combined. Gradually add the flour, starting with 1 1/2 cups, and mix until the dough comes together and is smooth and slightly sticky. Add more flour as needed, up to 2 cups total, to achieve a soft but not too sticky consistency.
4. Shape the gnocchi: Divide the dough into 4 equal parts. On a lightly floured surface, roll each part into a long rope about 1/2 inch thick. Cut the ropes into 1-inch pieces. Use a fork or gnocchi board to create ridges on each piece (optional).

5. Cook the gnocchi: Bring a large pot of salted water to a gentle boil. Add the gnocchi in batches, about 15-20 pieces at a time, and cook until they float to the surface, about 2-3 minutes. Remove with a slotted spoon and transfer to a plate.

To make the Tomato Sauce:

6. Prepare the sauce: In a large skillet, heat olive oil over medium heat. Add minced garlic and cook for 1 minute until fragrant. Add the diced tomatoes (with their juices), dried oregano, dried basil, salt, and pepper. Stir well and bring to a simmer. Cook for 10-15 minutes, stirring occasionally, until the sauce has thickened slightly.
7. Combine and serve: Add the cooked gnocchi to the tomato sauce in the skillet. Gently toss to coat the gnocchi evenly with the sauce. Cook for another minute or two until heated through.
8. Serve: Remove from heat and garnish with chopped fresh basil leaves and grated Parmesan cheese. Serve immediately.

Tips:

- Be gentle when mixing and shaping the gnocchi dough to avoid overworking it, which can make the gnocchi tough.
- Use a slotted spoon to transfer the cooked gnocchi directly from the boiling water to the sauce to prevent excess water from diluting the sauce.
- If the gnocchi dough feels too sticky, dust your hands and work surface lightly with flour.

This Tomato and Ricotta Gnocchi recipe offers a delicious blend of flavors and textures, perfect for a comforting homemade meal. Enjoy the pillowy gnocchi paired with the savory tomato sauce and creamy ricotta!

Tomato and Tuna Salad

Ingredients:

- 2 (5 oz / 140g each) cans of tuna in water or olive oil, drained
- 3 large tomatoes, chopped into bite-sized pieces
- 1/2 cucumber, diced
- 1/4 red onion, thinly sliced
- 1/4 cup Kalamata olives, pitted and sliced
- 1/4 cup fresh parsley, chopped
- 2 tablespoons extra virgin olive oil
- 1 tablespoon red wine vinegar or lemon juice
- Salt and pepper, to taste
- Optional: Crumbled feta cheese, for garnish

Instructions:

1. Prepare the salad base: In a large bowl, combine the chopped tomatoes, diced cucumber, thinly sliced red onion, Kalamata olives, and chopped parsley.
2. Add tuna: Flake the drained tuna into the bowl with the vegetables. Gently toss to combine, being careful not to break up the tuna too much.
3. Dress the salad: Drizzle extra virgin olive oil and red wine vinegar (or lemon juice) over the salad. Season with salt and pepper to taste. Toss again gently to coat all the ingredients evenly.
4. Serve: Transfer the Tomato and Tuna Salad to serving plates or a platter. Optionally, sprinkle with crumbled feta cheese for added flavor and creaminess.
5. Enjoy: Serve the salad immediately as a light and nutritious meal. It pairs well with crusty bread or as a side dish alongside grilled meats or fish.

Tips:

- You can customize this salad by adding other ingredients such as avocado slices, bell peppers, or even cooked quinoa or couscous for added texture.
- Adjust the dressing to your taste by adding more vinegar or lemon juice for acidity, or a touch of honey for sweetness.
- Make sure to use good quality canned tuna for the best flavor. You can choose tuna packed in water for a lighter option or in olive oil for added richness.

This Tomato and Tuna Salad recipe is perfect for a quick and healthy meal that's packed with protein and fresh flavors. Enjoy its simplicity and delicious combination of ingredients!

Tomato and Basil Pesto

Ingredients:

- 2 cups cherry tomatoes, halved
- 1 cup fresh basil leaves, packed
- 1/2 cup grated Parmesan cheese
- 1/4 cup pine nuts or walnuts, toasted
- 2 cloves garlic, minced
- 1/2 cup extra virgin olive oil
- Salt and pepper, to taste

Instructions:

1. Toast the nuts (if not already toasted): Heat a dry skillet over medium heat. Add the pine nuts or walnuts and toast, stirring frequently, until they are lightly golden and fragrant. Remove from heat and let them cool.
2. Prepare the pesto: In a food processor or blender, combine the cherry tomatoes, fresh basil leaves, grated Parmesan cheese, toasted nuts, and minced garlic. Pulse several times until the ingredients are finely chopped and combined.
3. Add olive oil: With the food processor running, slowly drizzle in the extra virgin olive oil until the pesto reaches your desired consistency. You may need to scrape down the sides of the processor bowl with a spatula and blend again to ensure everything is well incorporated.
4. Season: Taste the Tomato and Basil Pesto and season with salt and pepper to taste. Adjust the flavors as needed by adding more Parmesan cheese, basil, or olive oil.
5. Serve or store: Transfer the pesto to a jar or airtight container. Use it immediately or store it in the refrigerator for up to a week. If storing, drizzle a thin layer of olive oil on top of the pesto to help preserve its vibrant color.

Serving Suggestions:

- Toss Tomato and Basil Pesto with cooked pasta and garnish with additional Parmesan cheese and fresh basil.
- Use it as a spread on sandwiches or wraps, paired with fresh mozzarella and tomatoes for a Caprese-inspired sandwich.
- Drizzle over grilled chicken, fish, or vegetables for added flavor.

This Tomato and Basil Pesto recipe is easy to make and enhances dishes with its fresh, herbaceous flavor combined with the sweetness of tomatoes. Enjoy it in various ways to add a burst of summer goodness to your meals!

Tomato and Pepper Ratatouille

Ingredients:

- 2 tablespoons olive oil
- 1 onion, diced
- 3 cloves garlic, minced
- 1 red bell pepper, diced
- 1 yellow bell pepper, diced
- 1 medium eggplant, diced
- 2 zucchinis, diced
- 4 tomatoes, diced (or 1 can - 14.5 oz / 411g - diced tomatoes)
- 1 tablespoon tomato paste
- 1 teaspoon dried thyme (or 1 tablespoon fresh thyme leaves)
- 1 teaspoon dried basil (or 1 tablespoon fresh basil leaves, chopped)
- Salt and pepper, to taste
- Fresh parsley or basil, chopped, for garnish

Instructions:

1. Sauté onions and garlic: Heat olive oil in a large skillet or Dutch oven over medium heat. Add diced onion and sauté for 3-4 minutes until softened. Add minced garlic and cook for another minute until fragrant.
2. Cook bell peppers and eggplant: Add diced red and yellow bell peppers to the skillet. Cook for 5-6 minutes until they begin to soften. Add diced eggplant and cook for another 5 minutes, stirring occasionally.
3. Add zucchini and tomatoes: Stir in diced zucchini and tomatoes (with their juices). Cook for 5-7 minutes until the vegetables are tender and tomatoes start to break down.
4. Season and simmer: Add tomato paste, dried thyme, and dried basil (if using fresh, add it later). Stir well to combine. Season with salt and pepper to taste. Reduce heat to low, cover, and let it simmer for 15-20 minutes, stirring occasionally, to allow flavors to meld together.
5. Finish and garnish: Remove from heat. If using fresh basil, stir it in now. Taste and adjust seasoning if needed. Garnish with chopped fresh parsley or basil.
6. Serve: Tomato and Pepper Ratatouille can be served warm or at room temperature. It's delicious on its own or served over cooked pasta, rice, or with crusty bread.

Tips:

- For a richer flavor, you can roast the diced eggplant separately in the oven with a drizzle of olive oil until softened and slightly caramelized before adding to the skillet.
- Ratatouille develops more flavor as it sits, so it's great as leftovers or for meal prep.
- Customize the dish by adding other vegetables such as mushrooms, carrots, or spinach according to your preference.

This Tomato and Pepper Ratatouille recipe is a wonderful way to enjoy a variety of seasonal vegetables in a delicious and nutritious dish. It's hearty, comforting, and perfect for any time of year!

Tomato and Herbed Rice Pilaf

Ingredients:

- 1 cup long-grain white rice (such as basmati or jasmine)
- 1 tablespoon olive oil or butter
- 1 onion, finely chopped
- 2 cloves garlic, minced
- 1 can (14.5 oz / 411g) diced tomatoes, drained
- 1 3/4 cups vegetable broth or chicken broth
- 1 teaspoon dried thyme (or 1 tablespoon fresh thyme leaves)
- 1 teaspoon dried oregano (or 1 tablespoon fresh oregano leaves)
- Salt and pepper, to taste
- Fresh parsley or basil, chopped, for garnish

Instructions:

1. Prepare the rice: Rinse the rice under cold water until the water runs clear. This helps remove excess starch for fluffier rice when cooked.
2. Sauté aromatics: In a large skillet or saucepan, heat the olive oil or butter over medium heat. Add the chopped onion and cook for 3-4 minutes until softened. Add the minced garlic and cook for another minute until fragrant.
3. Add tomatoes and rice: Stir in the drained diced tomatoes and rice. Cook for 1-2 minutes, stirring constantly, to lightly toast the rice.
4. Simmer: Pour in the vegetable or chicken broth. Add dried thyme, dried oregano, salt, and pepper. Stir well to combine. Bring to a boil, then reduce heat to low. Cover and simmer for 15-20 minutes, or until the rice is tender and liquid is absorbed.
5. Fluff and garnish: Once the rice is cooked, remove from heat and let it sit covered for 5 minutes. Fluff the rice with a fork. Taste and adjust seasoning if needed.
6. Serve: Transfer the Tomato and Herbed Rice Pilaf to a serving dish. Garnish with chopped fresh parsley or basil before serving.

Tips:

- For extra flavor, you can add a pinch of crushed red pepper flakes for a hint of heat.
- Feel free to customize the pilaf with additional vegetables such as diced bell peppers or carrots.
- If using fresh herbs, add them towards the end of cooking or sprinkle them on top before serving for the freshest flavor.

This Tomato and Herbed Rice Pilaf is a versatile side dish that complements grilled meats, fish, or as part of a vegetarian meal. Enjoy its delicious blend of tomatoes, herbs, and fluffy rice!

Tomato and Basil Bruschetta

Ingredients:

- 4-5 ripe tomatoes, diced
- 1/4 cup fresh basil leaves, chopped (plus extra for garnish)
- 2 cloves garlic, minced
- 2 tablespoons extra virgin olive oil
- 1 tablespoon balsamic vinegar (optional)
- Salt and pepper, to taste
- 1 baguette or Italian bread, sliced
- Olive oil, for brushing

Instructions:

1. Prepare the tomatoes: In a medium bowl, combine the diced tomatoes, chopped fresh basil, minced garlic, extra virgin olive oil, and balsamic vinegar (if using). Season with salt and pepper to taste. Stir well to combine all the ingredients. Let the mixture sit at room temperature for about 15-20 minutes to allow the flavors to meld together.
2. Prepare the bread: Preheat the oven to 400°F (200°C). Arrange the bread slices on a baking sheet in a single layer. Brush both sides of the bread slices lightly with olive oil.
3. Toast the bread: Place the baking sheet in the preheated oven and toast the bread slices for about 5-7 minutes, or until they are golden brown and crispy. Remove from the oven and let them cool slightly.
4. Assemble the bruschetta: Spoon the tomato and basil mixture generously onto each toasted bread slice. Drizzle any remaining juices from the tomato mixture over the top. Garnish with additional chopped basil leaves.
5. Serve: Arrange the Tomato and Basil Bruschetta on a serving platter and serve immediately. Enjoy as a delicious appetizer or a light snack.

Tips:

- Use ripe tomatoes for the best flavor. Roma tomatoes or cherry tomatoes work well.
- You can customize the bruschetta by adding a sprinkle of shredded mozzarella cheese or a drizzle of balsamic glaze on top before serving.
- For a twist, you can grill the bread slices instead of toasting them in the oven for added smokiness.

This Tomato and Basil Bruschetta recipe is perfect for entertaining guests or enjoying as a quick and flavorful appetizer. Its simplicity highlights the freshness of the ingredients, making it a favorite dish during the summer months!

www.ingramcontent.com/pod-product-compliance
Lightning Source LLC
LaVergne TN
LVHW081608060526
838201LV00054B/2149